HOW THE CLERGY LIED

A JOURNALIST'S ACADEMIC REPORT ON LGBTQ AND BIBLICAL INTERPRETATION

D. L. DAY

ISBN - 979-8-9871396-5-3 - Paperback edition
ISBN- 979-8-9871396-6-0 - Hardback edition

———————

TRANSLATIONS OF THE BIBLE USED IN THE SERIES

AMPC - Amplified® Bible, Copyright © 1954, 1958, 1962, 1964, 1965, 1987 by The Lockman Foundation Used by permission. www.lockman.org"

ASV – HOLY BIBLE, AMERICAN STANDARD VERSION. *Public Domain*

ESV – THE HOLY BIBLE, ENGLISH STANDARD VERSION®, Copyright© 2001 by Crossway, a publishing ministry of Good News Publishers. Used by permission.

GNT - Good News Translation in Today's English Version- Second Edition Copyright © 1992 by American Bible Society. Used by Permission.

JB –JERUSALEM BIBLE Copyright© 1966, 1967, 1968 by Darton, Longmand & Todd LTD and Doubleday and Co. Inc. All rights reserved.

KJV – HOLY BIBLE, KING JAMES VERSION. *Public Domain.*

LITV - LITERAL TRANSLATION OF THE HOLY BIBLE, Copyright© 1976-2000 by Jay P. Green, Sr. Used by permission.

NAS – *NEW AMERICAN STANDARD BIBLE®,* *Copyright© 1960, 1962, 1963, 1968, 1971, 1972, 1973, 1975, 1977, 1995 by The Lockman Foundation. Used by permission.*

NIV – THE HOLY BIBLE, NEW INTERNATIONAL VERSION®. Copyright© 1973, 1978, 1984, 2011 by Biblica, Inc.™. Used by permission of Zondervan.

NLT – HOLY BIBLE, NEW LIVING TRANSLATION, Copyright © 1996,

Note that URL links included in references as an aid for further research were checked at publication. Due to the variability of internet sites, the accuracy of addresses may change over time.

All URL links listed were verified as of November, 2022 - January, 2023.

For Giordano Bruno
You knew the scorn of The Church and the truth of the stars.

CONTENTS

Now therefore why tempt ye God, to put a yoke upon the neck of the disciples, which neither our fathers nor we were able to bear. – St. Peter as quoted in Acts 15:10 (KJV)

PREFACE

Book Two of A Series of Two

Please also reference Book I, *Why the Clergy Lied: A Journalist's Academic Report on LGBTQ and Christianity.*

STILL BREAKING THE RULES

This book is part of a series of two. Book I, *Why the Clergy Lied: A Journalist's Academic Report on LGBTQ and Christianity*, covered the reasons behind centuries of untruths about LGBTQ inclusion and Christianity. This second book in the series covers how the clergy juggled Biblical translation, interpretation, and expository messaging to underpin the oppression of LGBTQ persons through much of Christian history.

There are numerous books on this subject. This is a different approach with a close look at the mechanisms of manipulation. It is a new approach that does not always abide by the obligations to play by strictly patriarchal rules.

In 1980 I gave a set of my writings about LGBTQ and the Bible to a friend who was a doctoral candidate in a fundamentalist divinity school. Weeks later I asked for his views. He simply returned the paper saying he had no reason to read it because God's word was infallible and deserved no such examination and no explanation of its meaning. At the time I was quite upset by his reaction.

Now I realize that exchange was laughable, given that the entire fundamentalist/evangelical movement is perpetuated by persons religious who spend hours on radio, television, social media, and in churches loudly proclaiming their interpretation of what the Bible actually says and means. The whole pattern of their hours of appearances in pulpits and all kinds of meetings and media is to read a verse of Scripture, then enthusiastically expound vociferously on what it means. There is a huge network that is streaming eisegesis all over the world, introducing individual bias in the interpretation of Scripture twenty-four hours a day every day on every type of media and claiming it is all without error.

The response from my friend was my first introduction to "The Rules." That term is used here in quotes simply because it summarizes the understanding of many of religion's participants about interpretations of the Bible. For centuries the Bible was not made available to the unwashed masses because of a belief they simply couldn't handle it intellectually.

GUARDING THE RULES

Although the Bible is now widely available, exegesis of it is still governed by some righteously imposed rules that are different for various cultures, denominations, and social circumstances. This book may break all of them. First, despite rather extensive theological experience and study, I'm writing this book as a retired Journalist. That of course violates rule number one: You must be a theologian to comment in-depth about the Bible and religion (unless, of course, you are an *anointed* fundamentalist).

Sometimes rules are bent to let in a few historians, but the field is still jealously guarded. Since the first introduction to this rulebook by my friend from the fundamentalist seminary in 1980, I've learned of the other existing strictures for understanding the Scriptures. They are applied variously (sometimes viciously) and differently by various sects. With an acknowledgment that this set of writings probably breaks them all, our list of *Patriarchal Rules for Biblical Interpretation* is included at the end of this book in Appendix i.

Acknowledging that historically there have been some subtle differences between fundamentalists, evangelicals, and neo-evangelicals, the author notes that the recent politicization of beliefs has blurred those lines making it more difficult to differentiate. In this book series, the terms will be used individually or interchangeably to reference those who believe in a fundamentalist interpretation of scripture and in proselytizing with their faith.

For those who may not have read Book One, a portion of the Chapter "Why the Proof Text Attacks" is included also here as a preface to provide context for subsequent reporting on the many tricks of Biblical translation and interpretation that served to perpetuate persecution of gay people. Those rules are included as an Appendix i in this volume.

1

THE WRONG QUESTION!

It's impossible to live 'according to the Bible,' as if the Bible were a uniform and unambiguous book of law or an infallible oracle. This is why it is always important to ascertain the premise and purpose of each reading and interpretation of the Bible. There's always an agenda behind any reading of the Bible: the more political that agenda, the more biased the reading. – Martti Nissinen

---

(This Chapter is repeated from Volume I in this series to provide context for persons who may not have read that volume.)

A significant departure from the usual arguments here is to say that the LGBTQ religious community has been responding for too long to the matter of "whether the Bible *condemns* homosexuality." It is the epitome of bad messaging and even worse theological discourse.

We are trying to answer the wrong question. That is the question designed by the torturers. No one generally widely broadcasts the questions:

- Does the Bible condemn eating steak rare?
- Does the Bible condemn divorce?
- Does the Bible condemn barren couples for having sex?
- Does the Bible condemn a straight pastor's spouse for giving oral sex?
- Does the Bible condemn loaning money at interest?

(There are lots of others also.)

The question LGBTQ Christians have been working for so many years to answer is a trick question that ignores all the other things the Bible may "condemn" when read literally and without context. Taken out of context the Bible can be read to condemn almost anything.

An LGBTQ-affirming church congregation handing out a pamphlet titled *"Does the Bible Condemn Homosexuality"* is like a seafood restaurant printing on the bottom of their lunch menu, *"Does the Bible Condemn Eating Shrimp?"* Maybe a donut shop could distribute, *"Does the Bible Condemn Obesity?"* By the time one got through a couple of pages of Biblical exegesis, it would be time to go back to work and skip lunch or breakfast.

The Old Testament condemns not being circumcised. No one is checking men's pants when they come into the church. A search won't find many books written on that topic. There are no church pamphlets asking, *"Does the Bible Condemn the Uncut Penis?"* No synod is holding endless dialogue over the question of the ordination of the "uncut" to the ministry.

When any church decides to quit offering communion to uncircumcised men, one can start to believe they are serious about the imposition of Old Testament laws. Paul dealt with that matter quite harshly, but his guidance is being ignored by some modern Christians, even while they use others of his comments (totally out of context) to condemn people.

The real question should be: **"Are LGBTQ people singled out and treated differently by those who quote the Bible?"** The answer to that question should be obvious to everyone and the resounding answer is "Yes." The next question must be "Why?"

This book, along with Book I in this series, will invest some time looking at that question. Some women have addressed a similar "wrong question" dilemma in their feminist liberation journey. In her book, *Wildfire: Igniting the Shevolution,* Sonya Johnson says she got tired of asking on behalf of women wanting to respond to oppression, "what should we do?" She writes, "I began to understand it was an unanswerable question because we can't postulate a new paradigm standing in and saturated by the old one."[1]

Religious oppressors have owned and controlled the church and religious dialogue for so many centuries it has created the paradigm suggesting LGBTQ people must knock at the gate to get in. There are pitifully shortcoming responses to our knocking. The "love the sinner not the sin" approach is popular with the Catholic church. "Homosexuality may not be a sin," they have decided, but "homosexual acts" are. A similar approach is taken by the Church of Jesus Christ of Latter Day Saints and others. It is a cheap ticket out of the dilemma for them.

If we are asking the wrong question founded in the wrong paradigm, the real issue is that too many churches have chosen to demonstrably treat LGBTQ people differently in the application of Scripture and social expectations. Let's talk about why?

A FREE GOAT IN THE WILD

The answer is Scapegoating. This term is taken from, of course, Leviticus. One can find there (after all the proscriptions and rules and potential for transgressions) a simple out to purge sin. Aaron is instructed by God to prepare a scapegoat, cast all the sins of Israel on it, and send it off into the wilderness, thus carrying the sins away. Easy breezy right? Leviticus 16:

8: Aaron shall cast lots for the two goats one lot for the LORD and the other lot for the scapegoat.
9: Then Aaron shall offer the goat on which the lot for the LORD fell and make it a sin offering.
10: "But the goat on which the lot for the scapegoat fell shall be presented alive before the LORD to make atone-ment upon it to send it into the wilderness as the scapegoat.
21: Then Aaron shall lay both of his hands on the head of the live goat and confess over it all the iniquities of the sons of Israel and all their transgressions regarding all their sins; and he shall lay them on the head of the goat and send it away into the wilderness by the hand of a man who stands in readiness.
22: "The goat shall bear on itself all their iniquities to a solitary land; and he shall release the goat in the wilderness.
26: The one who released the goat as the scapegoat shall wash his clothes and bathe his body with water; then after-

ward he shall come into the camp. (New American Standard Bible)

There we have it. Heap your sins on that scapegoat, send it off into the wilderness, wash your hands, and be done with it. Now you can enter the temple tripping happily, cleansed of your filthy awfulness while another innocent goat burns on the altar.

The whole concept of sacrifice comes from the influence of centuries of pagan religions' belief that blood sacrifices quelled the anger of the Gods or were somehow a gift to win the gods' favor. How ironic that a modern society that is so appalled about indigenous shaman practitioners throwing virgins into a volcano to appease the gods, and so shocked by <u>any</u> idea of human sacrifice, would celebrate an entire Christian religion based on exactly that practice. It is a whole theme of bloody sacrifice of the pure to appease an angry god as compensation for some offense.

Scapegoating has become known in psychology as the method of using (an) innocent person(s) to relieve a person or group of their guilt and its consequences. One example can be the use of Jews by the Nazis to blame them for the failure of the regime in Germany after World War One. Another already cited in this book; King Philip IV of France, whose finances and kingdom were struggling, blamed the Muslims, the Jews, the Templars, and anyone he could find to charge with "sodomy."

So why would Leviticus be used for scapegoating LGBTQ people? Think about it. The Levitical Law was a stringent set of rules for righteousness. One can ignore most of it, point to those sins most positioned as somehow awful (like a magician distracting our attention), assume one's own sin is not that bad, righteously wash the hands, and go dancing through the holy tabernacle as pure as a new snowfall. All the while a goat plods off into oblivion with the sin load.

Many religions are like electricity in that they must have a positive and a negative polarity to function. When you get in touch with both, you are connected to the circuit. For there to be redemption, there must be transgression. Many religions can't exist without that counter-positioned combination. When there is a greater perception of transgression, the greater the believers' recognition of the power of redemption.

(Recently an evangelical proponent bragged to this author that their church's guest speaker for the week had been a "felon." Glory!)

This is the whole basis of the destitute sinner's confession and the perception of "power in the blood of Jesus." It is the entire foundation of *Original Sin* and of evangelicalism. Referencing the electricity analogy one can say, churches just need to keep scapegoats as a good solid connection to negative ground, or the preaching has nowhere to go.

The church has in the past found revivalist success in mass movements strictly by having an unredeemed "other" to reject. Perhaps this is a manifestation of an abandonment of the "unwanted self." In the words of Eric Hoffer,

> a mass movement, particularly in its active, revivalistic phase, appeals not to those intent on bolstering and advancing cherished self, but to those who crave to be rid of an unwanted self. A mass movement attracts and holds a following, not because it can satisfy the desire for self-advancement, but because it can satisfy the passion for self-renunciation.[2]

The relationship between LGBTQ and the ultra-conservative church is, clearly and simply, one of scapegoating. What else could explain the huge divergence between how Scripture is interpreted on a stand-alone basis for an isolated group cut out of the general population like what has happened to LGBTQ folks?

What else could explain an entire body in a religious synod (made up of theologians who have to know better from a Scriptural and historical standpoint) voting against the admission of LGBTQ people to their Christian fellowship? They simply cast lots to choose the goat.

The popular concept is "the church has to draw the line somewhere." The question churches should be asking is not "does the Bible condemn homosexuality?" The question is "why are LGBTQ people 'the line?'" How did the LGBTQ community draw the lot to have Scripture applied differently and be the scapegoat to bear away the guilt of the would-be holy?

A famous quote from Lyndon Johnson in an interview with Bill Moyers captures the objective of the concept pretty well:

> If you can convince the lowest white man he's better than the best colored man, he won't notice you're picking his pocket. Hell, give him somebody to look down on and he'll empty his pockets for you.[3]

One can think about that and apply it to the money machine that is some modern churches. Scapegoating is a highly profitable concern. Redemption can be so much more valuable when it is compared to the pitiful condition of the unwashed and unredeemed.

Scholar René Girard was the originator of "Mimetic Theory" and a refiner of the "Scapegoat" concept. Mimesis refers to conflict occurring when human rivals compete to differentiate themselves from each other. Girard conducted a great deal of research and commentary on Scapegoating. He tells us:

> When human groups divide and become fragmented during a period of malaise and conflicts, they may come to a point where they are reconciled again at the expense of a victim. Observers nowadays realize without difficulty, unless they belong to the persecuting group, that this victim is not really responsible for what he or she is accused of doing.
>
> The accusing group, however, views the victim as guilty by

virtue of a contagion like what we find in scapegoat rituals. The members of this group accuse their "scapegoat" with great fervor and sincerity.[4]

No amount of argument of Scriptural meaning is going to lift the blame from a scapegoat. Girard also pointed out: "If you scapegoat someone it's a third party that will be aware of it. It won't be you. Because you will believe you are doing the right thing."

As declared in this book, it may be a member of the oppressor class who is most successful in the validation of efforts to free the oppressed. It's a matter of some brave person standing to point out the innocence of the scapegoat.

It is a greater impact with a more impactful outcome when it is a member of the oppressor class who is pointing to the oppression and claiming it's undeserved. There is, however, a good bit of risk in that for the bearer of the declaration.

Importantly, the key to the whole scapegoating power structure is the assumed guilt of the goat. This is particularly poignant in light of the comparison to Biblical origins. The goat that was deemed by the priests to be "innocent" was slaughtered, cut up, and burned.

The "guilty" goat was released free into the wild, but in the minds of the congregants was turned over to the Devil. In the wilderness, the goat was likely to have been eaten by predators. (It would be nice to imagine that, what are now those beautiful, flowing-mane mountain goats that can climb straight up a rock face, are somehow the descendants of those ancient and innocent scapegoats.)

One could argue the one thing LGBTQ people have going for us is being free in the wild. Maybe some don't want to give that up. Some churches would still argue in favor of the "turned over to the Devil" part.

Fundamentalists attempt to declare the existence of a bright red line between themselves and the unwashed sinners of the world. The line of separation seems to glow brighter in relevance to the nature of the sin and depravation one's doctrine may decide to highlight, as well as the amount of perceived righteousness on the holy side. It is the line that declares the righteous more sanctified and special, worthy of all kinds of honor and blessing. None want to let go of the line, because it defines the occupants of both sides.

It can be said the whole concept of an innocent victim being sacrificed, while another bearing the sins of all is set free, forms a good part of the basis for the post-Constantine Christian religion. Considering that the freed goat was innocent too, the only guilt that comes into the picture is that shed by those who believed their sins were heaped upon the scapegoat and carried away.

Nowhere in the Bible does it say Abraham (or anybody else) was instructed to search around for a sinful goat. The self-righteous person's whole redemption theory unravels with any revelation it was only their sins the scapegoat was bearing and not its own. Jesus and Paul both said the same thing, but we paraphrase here: "Be careful who you accuse because you are condemning them of your own sin."

In talking about sacrifice for sin, one must recognize that the goat that was killed and grilled, as well as the one sent outside the gate, were both without sin of their own. They were equally innocent victims. One was symbolically turned over to God, and one to the Devil. The choice was not theirs, and they were never guilty of anything. If Christ symbolizes one, he must symbolize both.

If God no longer demands the burnt offering sacrifice, then God no longer demands that an innocent victim bear our sins by being ostracized. We, and both forms of sacrificial symbols, are all living under grace. This was Christ's overarching message. This was Paul's message he kept coming back to. Problem is, if it quits compartmentalizing, prioritizing, and punishing sin, the Christian church as most people know it today (post-Constantine and post-Augustine Christianity) goes away.

To Christians, staking out a scapegoat should be considered antithetical to the idea of grace and Christ being sacrificed for sins. Did Christ's blood serve to appease an angry God's wrath against humankind, or did it serve to herald the victory of love over archaic vengeance and sacrifice? Did it replace an era of transference of guilt to an innocent other, or did it signify the victory of grace over guilt? Was it to cure a mistake at Eden? Many think not.

One reason LGBTQ people are left waiting at the church gate is the potential for a challenge to the entire *Original Sin* and *Redemption* doctrines of the Christian religion. Don't expect the money-raising prosperity gospel believers to embrace LGBTQ people, no matter how convincing our approach to Scripture may be. To do so breaks the connection to the negative ground and short circuits the entire redemption circuitry.

It is only the fear of a horrible incursion of sin and evil in the world that drives the hallelujah revival van. If the goat is searched out in the wild and determined to have been innocent all along, the whole fundamentalists' concept of holier than thou, and somehow "purer," comes crashing down. Again, in the words of Girard, "A scapegoat remains effective as long as we believe in its guilt."[5]

Daniel Walden in a commentary for Catholics says this:

> to impose a foreign life story on an icon of God is to read another person through our sin and the lies that sin has taught us. It is sin—and we have so sinned—against them and against the God who made them. What we really owe them is a new beginning.[6]

All the preaching of some fundamentalists about "prosperity Gospel" with God heaping blessings for those who shun sin starts to come unraveled with the demise of self-imposed or comparative holiness. Their belief necessarily creates a situation in which amplifying the "guilt" of the scapegoat enhances the sense of right-eousness and resulting success in life for the "prosperity" Christian.

This seems to form the basis for a Dominionist idea that God is shifting wealth from the "evil" to the "righteous." It could turn out, however, to be the signs of the last gasp of fundamentalism.

In the words of Hoffer, "When a mass movement begins to attract people who are interested in their individual careers it is a sign that it has passed its vigorous stage; that it is no longer engaged in molding a new world but in possessing and preserving the present. It ceases then to be a movement and becomes an enterprise."[7] One should probably expect that the faster the enterprise begins to sink the more frantic will be the blame of the scapegoats.

Our examination of Scriptural arguments in this book is done with the full realization that the final religious decision-making in churches and many peoples' lives has very little to do with Scripture. It has more to do with how people frame the LGBTQ/religion story in the context of their prejudices.

The framing of LGBTQ living as life-threatening, wicked, and contrary to societal well-being may destroy lives, but it grows churches. It rides the wave of a scapegoat group dynamic and underpins the atonement meme. It completes the positive/negative redemption circuit.

2

THE NAKED GUY IN THE GARDEN

any form of discrimination against homosexuals must be rejected
as has been required by scholarly requirements for some time. –
A statement from German Roman Catholic Bishops in 2021

LGBTQ people have long been quite accepting of the overall
Christian positioning of what the Bible is and how it ought to be
read and understood. The Bible is not as it has generally been

described to us. As will be demonstrated here, there are many misrepresentations about the origins and nature of Scripture that have been perpetuated by clergy and theologians who know they are withholding the truth but conceal that knowledge so they can uphold their claims of inerrancy and Biblical authority.

In other words, sometimes some churches have lied to us about the Bible. Not always are they blatant, bald-faced lies, but certainly lies of omission of important information that might raise doubts. This writing will carefully consider *motivations* for Scriptural interpretation *and* misinterpretation.

PROOF TEXT IN CONTEXT

Recent revealing evidence about Scripture comes from theological think tank and academic stronghold, The Wijngaards Institute for Catholic Research. The organization issued in 2021 an important release describing how they have been coordinating an interdisciplinary panel of academics over a period of two years to produce a research report evaluating the morality of same-sex relationships from within the Catholic and overall Christian traditions. The study included an extensive exercise in Bible exegesis.

This was the first such report to bring together and assess the most recent peer-reviewed research on the biblical passages used to condemn same-sex relationships. Much of that crucial research has only been published as recently as March 2020 and so is still only known within academic circles. The release of the report said:

> While the report also examines scientific and sociological evidence, much of it is devoted to recent groundbreaking studies on the most important so-called "clobber texts" in the Bible:
>
> Leviticus 18:22 and 20:13 are popularly believed to be the most explicit and general condemnation of same-sex relationships. Our study can confirm that the traditional interpretation is based on a mistranslation.

On the contrary, those verses only refer to specific kinds of male same-sex sexual activity (specifically, adultery and incest) and none condemns same-sex relationships in general. Indeed, the fact that the prohibition addressed a specific type of activity suggests same-sex relationships outside the forbidden category were viewed as permissible.

Also, Romans 1:26-27 is misinterpreted as new research has convincingly revealed

There is no condemnation anywhere in the Bible of female same-sex relationships, and of consensual and faithful same-sex relationships in general.

From the point of view of the natural sciences, it can be affirmed that homosexuality is a "natural variation within the range of human sexuality"

Those who seek to exclude LGBTQ from religious communities base their beliefs on several Scriptures they quote individually to prove their point. In so doing, they use a technique of Biblical interpretation called, "proof texting." It's the same technique used to support other forms of bigotry. Quotes from the Bible are still used today to support discrimination against women and racial minorities. There was a time when some ministers even used Biblical passages to support the moral correctness of slavery. The Ku Klux Klan has been known to quote from the Bible. Even Satan is quoted in the Bible as quoting the Bible and using a proof text approach to Scripture.

Proof texting is the use of a single Scripture that seems to pertain to a certain topic as proof of God's opinion concerning that topic. Those persons who use proof texts to support their points of view frequently ignore these things:

- The cultural setting of the original Scripture

- The original meaning of the language at the time it was written
- The overall messages that surround it and appear throughout the Bible

To better understand how proof texting works and why it may lead to the misrepresentation of Scripture, let's take a look at a rather exaggerated example of the method as applied to a set of Scriptures. Suppose someone were to use the Bible to prove Jesus was hounded by the media everywhere he went. (Remember proof texting will disregard the true meaning of the language, the context as related to surrounding Scripture, and the historical context.)

Look at the woman with the "issue of blood" who approached Jesus by acting like she was part of the media: "When she had heard of Jesus came in *the press* behind and touched his garment."

Mark 5 verse 30 says Jesus "turned him about in *the press*." (KJV)

In Luke are other references to "*the press*" following Jesus:

Then came to him his mother and his brethren and could not come at him for *the press*. (Luke 8: 19 – KJV)

And he sought to see Jesus who he was; and could not for *the press* because he was of little stature. (Luke 19: 3 – KJV)

Of course, it's ridiculous to believe that these passages refer to the media. The media as it is known today did not exist in Jesus' time. "*The press*" in the King James version and the language of the time of its writing refers to the press of the crowd. That doesn't say Scripture was in error if one reads it thinking that there were media around Jesus. It does say that the interpretation was in error because it didn't consider all of the factors that were needed to properly understand its meaning in light of the time it was written. This would include the historical context of the reference, the language at the time of the translation, and the measured understanding in the context of "*the press*" in modern language and practice.

The reader would have made a blatant error that was easy to spot, but there are much more subtle errors being made by some of those who claim they are preaching the truth based on the "inerrancy" (without error) of Scripture. What those persons are claiming is an unerring understanding and inerrant interpretation of Scripture. If I as the author here were to claim Jesus was followed by the media, I could point to the inerrancy of Scripture all I wanted, and it still wouldn't prove Jesus was followed by the media. It would only prove that I was pretty much an idiot. This is just a simple example to demonstrate everyone to whatever degree, applies some context to their reading of Scripture.

One fascinating variation in Scripture is pointed out by Karmen Michael Smith in his groundbreaking book *Holy Queer: The Coming Out of Christ.*

The translators seemed to struggle somewhat with the idea the disciple "whom Jesus loved" was at the Last Supper reclining on Jesus breast.[1] The differences in Scripture versions are a little stunning:

> Now there was leaning on Jesus' bosom one of his disciples, whom Jesus loved. (KJV)
> The disciple Jesus loved was sitting next to Jesus at the table (NLT)
> One of them, the disciple whom Jesus loved, was reclining next to him (NIV)
> One of his disciples, whom Jesus loved, was reclining at table at Jesus side (ESV)

As you see, one translation goes so far as to allow someone to believe if they wanted that the *table* was at Jesus side. It appears a Greek word for bosom may have been totally (and perhaps intentionally) overlooked or treated quite differently by some of the translators. There is also quite a difference between "*the* disciple whom Jesus loved" and "one of his *disciples*, whom Jesus loved." God forbid anybody gets the wrong impression.

The Bible is a book that has to be interpreted just as any book. Preachers do it every week. That is not to say the Bible isn't distinctive; it has great distinction and uniqueness. It is positioned in our world as the word of God. One should distinguish between the "word of God" and the "words of God."

There is no overall declaration the originators of the Bible were claiming to be passing on the actual words of God. Jeremiah for example says he is issuing "the words of Jeremiah to whom the word of God came." (Jeremiah 1:1-2.) Paul makes a clear distinction at times that proclamations are simply coming from him.

The writers of the Bible did not know they were writing the Bible. They did know they were at times compiling stories for very specific reasons. As an example, one can look at the story of Ruth.

CLEANING UP A LITTLE ANCESTRY

We in church school were trained to believe the *Book of Ruth* is just a sweet story of one woman relative's devotion to another. What a nice nod to women that such a lovely account of friendship and relationship is in one of only two books in the Scripture named after women. Truth is, at times the writings in the Bible cast stories in a way to create enhanced public relations for leaders.

There is reason to believe the *Book of Ruth* was written to delicately reframe and position the inconvenient fact that King David's great-grandmother was not Israelite and may have had a questionable marriage situation. Curiously, even though other Bible heroes have heavy descriptions of genealogy, accounts of David's family history in Scripture are brief and shortchange his maternal lineage.

The *Book of Ruth* tells how the Moabite woman by that name bonded with Naomi an Israelite. While the book can be read as a wonderful story of devotion. It can also be seen as a way to dramatically depict Ruth in the act of leaving her Moabite roots behind and clinging to Naomi's Israelite culture (a convert as it were). Marrying Moabites was strictly forbidden for Israelites. This is what needed to be cleaned up about King David's heritage.

In quoting the famous statement of Ruth to Naomi "thy God shall be my God," the writing depicts Ruth as apparently rejecting Chemosh the god of Moab in favor of Naomi's God Yahweh. The story of Ruth can be seen as a repositioning of what some saw as David's tainted ancestry by clearing any suspicion about his Moabite great-grandmother Ruth.[2]

In addition to recounting the conversion of Ruth, the book sets out to unravel her compliance with a set of laws by which the two women avoided complicated issues regarding requirements to marry a relative of a dead husband, and how they sorted through laws about estates. The whole writing serves to clear up any skewed perceptions that statutes, customs, and precedents may have been broken in the subsequent family ties of Naomi and Ruth as an ancestor of King David.[3]

It is interesting to note that in Matthew 1:1-16 there are only five women listed in the genealogy of Jesus. Ruth is among them. The characterization of Ruth serves as a good example of how steps were taken to influence the understanding of history in support of the purity of the faith. The real intent of the book to do a little cleaning job on King David's family history seems to have been obscured in church schools all along.

BUT, NAKED?!

The traditional churches have misread, misled, and just ignored into oblivion certain Scriptures and practices of the early church that just didn't strike the leaders as convenient in their world. For example, most of us were never told in church that when the Romans arrested Jesus in the Garden of Gethsemane at night, he was in the company of a young man who was naked, "except for a linen cloth wrapped around him." Here it is in Mark:14:51-52 (KJV) as it describes Jesus' arrest:

> And there followed him a certain young man having a linen cloth
> cast about his naked body; and the young men laid hold on him:
> And he left the linen cloth and fled from them naked. (Mark
> 14:51-52 – KJV)

Many Christians went through scores of Easter celebrations and various reenactments of the passion of Jesus and never heard of this Scripture. No one ever went to an "Easter Sunrise Service" to see a reenactment of some naked guy running out of the garden. (It might have amped up the attendance if we had.)

Why did it not happen, because the guardians of church tradition didn't want us to get the "wrong idea." They were afraid we would ask, "Who was that guy, and what was he doing out there in the garden at night with a little cloth around him?" (The King James Version says "naked" not once, but twice.) Church leaders didn't have a good explanation for it, so they just left it out. It was not a part of the traditional narrative of the church. That is how a lot of Scripture is obscured for us with the assumption we can't handle it. "Let's just skip over the naked garden guy," church leaders may say.

One could claim with great certainty that the following statement is entirely Biblical: Jesus was arrested after being betrayed by a kiss from a man while in a public garden at night accompanied by a naked young man with a little cloth wrapped around him. This followed a dinner during which the male "disciple he loved" reclined on his bosom.

That is all Scriptural. How one understands that presentation of Scripture and what one assumes from it depends a great deal on context, translation, and nuance. Even though it is one hundred percent Biblical, the mere citation in sequence can be considered by some to be quite heretical.

UNDERSTANDING SCRIPTURE IN CONTEXT

Some of the Bible was carried for years from campfire storyteller to campfire storyteller before ever being written down. Other pieces were the subject of literal bloody wars between factions to determine what the accepted wording of Scripture would be, or what Scriptures would be included in whichever denomination's Bible. Some were compiled to hold a religion together in the face of a highly competitive environment of celebration of other deities. Several things must be known to better understand the meaning of a verse of Scripture:

1. One must know the social context in which the words of the text were written. What is the society what is the culture out of which these writings have come to us? It is in the broadest sense the whole of the original society that supplies the context.

2. One must know what specific situation may have prompted each text. In the case of Paul for instance he was writing to specific churches in specific places about specific local societal and political problems. We need to know what those problems were if we are to understand Paul's response to them.

3. One must know how the text relates to the overall view of the writer. What is the meaning, considering other things that the same writer tells us?

4. One must know how a text relates theologically, that is how it can be seen in light of the whole message of the Bible and how it relates overall to every other text. How does it fit into the overall picture of Biblical faith? The approach that is pertinent to the nature of the Bible itself is to inquire into these kinds of contexts out of which the specific texts have come.[4]

5. One must contemplate who may have actually written
    the text or influenced it somehow during the writing
    and translating.

This writing will take a journalist's approach to look at scholarship and considerations available for all four of these methods for
evaluating commonly proof texted Scriptures.

INTERPRETATION IS COMMON AND MANDATORY

Everyone to some degree interprets the Bible in light of the
language and the time in which it was written. Even the most rigid
Bible-pounding conservative preacher uses this approach to an
extent. For example, the Bible says, "If thy right eye offend thee
pluck it out. If thy right hand offend thee cut it off." (Matt.5: 29-30
– KJV) You don't see very many one-eyed, one-armed fundamentalist preachers.

This is not because their hands or eyes never in their lives
offended them. It's because they consider this Scripture, at least, in
the light of the time it was written and in the context of
surrounding Scripture. It is their conscious choice to interpret
Scripture as actually not demanding body part severing in modern
times.

According to Deuteronomy, if a man marries a woman and
finds out she is not a virgin she can be stoned to death.

> then they shall bring the girl out to the doorway of her father's
> house, and the men of her city shall stone her to death, because
> she has committed a disgraceful sin in Israel by playing the pros-
> titute in her father's house; so you shall eliminate the evil from
> among you. (Deuteronomy 22:21 - NAS)

If everyone followed inerrancy, there would be a lot of people
getting stoned.

There are almost a hundred instances of "ass" in the Bible. Even the person who most rabidly clings to the thought the Bible must be taken at face value word-for-word from the King James version will admit to you that anytime the Bible talks about an "ass" it means a donkey. That is critical historical interpretation of Scripture. It is considering the Scripture in light of the language and cultural setting of the time in which it was written and setting aside flaws in translation to modern languages.

It's not a question then of whether a person is willing to use these techniques in interpreting Scripture. To a certain extent, everyone does. The question becomes whether a person is willing to put the techniques to work on all of Scripture and not just to the question of whether an ass is a donkey (or a burro, or a butt).

The New Testament as it is known today never existed in this form in singular ancient original manuscripts. Those now trying to translate Scripture must draw on a myriad of possibilities for what comes closest to original texts.

There are variously augmented, error-filled copies over centuries. Before the invention of the printing press, the New Testament was copied thousands of times by hand. Not only are there Greek copies but thousands of versions by scribes captured in Latin and a multitude of other ancient languages.[5] There is nowhere any verified original text. Many of the versions we've inherited contain additions and subtractions no doubt influenced by centuries of church bias and politics.

In his brilliant book, *A History of the Bible: The Book and Its Faiths,* John Barton (a theologian who served as the Professor of the Interpretation of Holy Scripture at the University of Oxford in England for twenty-three years) says the Bible should be considered fully supportive of neither the Christian nor the Jewish religion:

> In truth, there are no versions of either Christianity or Judaism that correspond point for point to the contents of the Bible, which is often not what it has been made into and read as.

In Christianity for example, there are absolutely central doctrines such as that of the Trinity that are almost entirely absent from the New Testament; conversely, there are central ideas in the New Testament such as St Paul's theory of 'salvation by grace through faith' that, at least until the Reformation, were never part of official orthodoxy at all and even now are not in the creeds.[6]

There are no original versions of Biblical texts. Scholars today have available for research over five thousand Greek manuscripts purported to be parts of the New Testament. They range from very small pieces to rather large scrolls. None are original texts from Biblical times. The manuscripts only date back to small fragments from the early second century. Among the New Testament manuscripts, one can find from 200,000 to 400,000 variations in what they are saying, with a greater number of variants than there are words in the New Testament itself. [7]

What exactly is inerrant? Which is the inerrant version from the 200-to-400 thousand? This is further confounded by the fact that Jesus and many of those with him spoke Aramaic and the bulk of the New Testament was written, organized, and assembled in Greek. It was all an exercise in memory, translation, and extrapolation.

The research organization Westar Institute has done an extensive examination of the historical Jesus and the influence of the followers of Jesus, from his ministry, until the appearance of Constantine over 200 years later. In a book reporting on their research on the early Jesus movement, the authors have this warning about translation:

The Italian proverb "Traduttore, traditore" (to translate is to betray) sums up the problem with translations. All translations are mistranslations. Readers need to keep this in mind. Mistranslation is not deliberate but results from the inevitable fact that words and grammar do not have an exact correspondence between languages.

So-called word-for-word or literal translations are actually impossible. Translation is always interpretation, whether or not it is admitted to be such. Also, a language over time shifts and changes, which is why we always need new translations.[8]

Persons who want to make stand-alone, word-for-word use of the Bible and claim inerrancy for that method need to take a closer look at Scripture. For those who want to do an interesting exercise to examine some conflicting texts in Scripture, start with the example to compare Ezra 2 (**KJV**) with Nehemiah 7 (**KJV**). These list some people who came out of Babylonian captivity. One might say several things about the significant disparity in the numbers listed there.

It could be said that time passed between them and people forgot. It could be said there was a different count and understanding of what the numbers ought to be. What can't be substantiated is that both sets of numbers are "inerrant." They are close, it is interesting there are two accounts, but they can't both be without doubt, can't both be divinely precise.

There are also similar occurrences in the New Testament. Of particular interest are the differing accounts of a number of events. In Matthew, for example, the word of Jesus' birth comes to Joseph, and in Luke, to Mary. Matthew's account of the Lord's Prayer has seven petitions: Luke's only five. Matthew has eight beatitudes; Luke has four beatitudes and four woes.[9]

The Gospels don't agree on what happened at Jesus' resurrection. Those narratives are found in Matthew 28, Mark 16, Luke 24, and John 20–21. There are quite differing accounts:

Matthew

- There were two Marys at the tomb.

- There was a great earthquake.
- The stone door was rolled away by an angel *after* the women got there.
- An angel spoke to the women.
- They were then met and told by Jesus to tell the disciples he would meet them in Galilee.
- Women told the disciples.
- Jesus met disciples in Galilee

Mark

- There were two Marys and Salome at the tomb.
- The stone was already rolled away before they arrived.
- A young man met and spoke to them.
- They were told Jesus would meet the disciples in Galilee.
- The poor lil ole women were just so "amazed" and afraid they "trembled" and "fled" and didn't tell anybody.
- Jesus later appeared to Mary Magdalene (who told others, but they didn't believe her).
- Then Jesus appeared to two others, then eleven in Galilee

Luke

- There were two Marys, Joanna, and a group of other unknown women at the tomb.
- Stone was already rolled away.
- Women were met by two men.
- They were told to remember what Jesus had told them in Galilee.
- The disciples ultimately saw Jesus in Jerusalem after he had met Cleopis and another man in Emmaus.

John

- There was one Mary at the tomb.
- Stone was already rolled away.
- Mary was met by two angels and Jesus.
- Mary did tell the disciples
- They met Jesus in Jerusalem and later at the sea of Tiberias where they all went fishing.[10]

Curiously, any comparison of these accounts featuring the purported witnesses to the most important event in Christian history would never even stand up in a small-town police interrogation room. Of course, witness accounts can be expected to vary, especially if they are written a century or two after an event by someone who wasn't there.

Is this evidence the resurrection of Christ didn't happen? No. The purpose here is not to disparage the event, but simply to say there are varying accounts comprised over at least a couple of hundred years and evolving through any number of authors, scribes, understandings, copying, interpretations, and translations. Precisely which one is inerrant? To say they are all inerrant word-for-word is unreasonable.

The New Testament books of the Bible are not in agreement on who Jesus' grandfather through Joseph was. In fact, the Matthew and Luke accounts of his genealogy differ all the way back to King David. Which is inerrant?

The Gospels contain three different versions of what were Jesus' last words on the cross. Judas either went right out and hanged himself after betraying Jesus, or he bought a farm, fell down in a field, and his guts burst open, depending on what book you're reading.

Consider the Biblical contradictions about prayer:

> I will therefore that men pray everywhere, lifting up holy hands, without wrath and doubting. (1 Timothy 2:8 – KJV)
>
> Pray without ceasing. (1 Thessalonians 5:17 – KJV)
>
> But thou when thou prayest, enter into thy closet, and when thou hast shut thy door, pray to thou Father which is in secret. (Matthew 6:5-8 – KJV)
>
> Be not rash with thy mouth, and let not thine heart be hasty to utter anything before God: for God is in heaven, and thou upon the earth: therefor let they words be few. (Ecclesiastes 5:2 – KJV)

What is a person to do about praying?

With all of these conflicts of fact in mind, one can surmise there probably wasn't a stenographer present writing down in red ink every word Jesus spoke. We can note that Martin Luther wanted to just dump the book of James from teaching in schools because it contradicted Paul's belief about whether good works are necessary for salvation.

He proclaimed, "Therefore St. James' epistle is an epistle of straw compared to these others, for it has nothing of the nature of the Gospel about it."[11]

Bart D. Ehrman is a Distinguished Professor of Religious Studies at the University of North Carolina Chapel Hill and is a leading authority on the Bible and the life of Jesus. He is the author of more than twenty books including three New York Times bestsellers. In his book *Forged: Writing in the Name of God--Why the Bible's Authors Are Not Who We Think They Are*, Ehrman provides strong evidence that just under half of the books in the New Testament are not written by the authors that are claimed. In his book, Ehrman poses and answers the questions:

> That some of Paul's letters were not actually written by Paul but by someone claiming to be Paul? That Peter's letters were not written by Peter? That James and Jude did not write the books that bear their names? Or—a somewhat different case as we will see—that the Gospels of Matthew Mark Luke and John were not actually written by Matthew Mark Luke and John? Scholars for over a hundred years have realized that this is the case.
>
> The authors of some of the books of the New Testament were not who they claimed to be or who they have been supposed to be.[12]

In opposing the deuterocanonical books of the Bible (included by Catholics but not in the Protestant Bible), Protestants have often pointed to the idea there are inconsistencies in the "apocryphal" books. However, there is little acknowledgment of the general Bible inconsistencies in the Protestant Bible when inerrancy is imposed.

Protestants leave out of their Bible some books the Catholic Church, the Eastern Orthodox Church, the Oriental Orthodox Churches, and the Assyrian Church of the East include in their Bibles as canonical books of the Old Testament. Here is a list of the books of the Bible excluded by the Protestant version of the Scripture:

In the Bible of the Catholic Church and the Eastern Orthodox Church

- Tobit
- Judith
- Baruch
- 1 Maccabees
- 2 Maccabees

- Sirach (sometimes called Ecclesiasticus)
- Wisdom
- Additions to the books of Esther Daniel and Baruch

Additionally in the Bible only for the Eastern Orthodox Church

- Prayer of Manasseh
- 1 Esdras
- 2 Esdras
- Psalm 151
- 3 Maccabees
- 4 Maccabees (an appendix)
- Note: The Book of Revelations is included but not read in most churches

Without getting too confusing (which it is), one can just say that the shopping done over the centuries as to what to include in the Bible mostly took place hundreds of years after Jesus. It evolved into primarily Latin and Greek versions, of which there were many. St. Jerome gathered from a myriad of Latin sources, and one Greek version and worked to contribute to the Latin Vulgate (about 386 CE). Part of the source for the Vulgate was the Septuagint for the Old Testament. Jerome used numerous versions of translations (mostly Latin) for the New Testament. He had studied Greek and Hebrew for only a few years.

It wasn't until the 1800s that the Apocryphal books were dropped by most Protestant Churches. Led by the Church of England and Luther, this process was later pushed by the Presbyterians and the Puritans. All were willing to get into a heated debate on what was inerrant.

Just as some major denominations cut books out of other denominations' Bibles, some other Gospels that may have been equally as legitimate were never even allowed to see the light of day as a part of the post-Constantine church.

"Seeing the light of day" is a meaningful phrase in the modern quest to find ancient texts. Researchers using UV light are still finding ancient Syriac versions of New Testament scripture that appear under layers of other writings. Because writing parchment was scarce, scribes sometimes used a method to erase the visible ink and write on top of it. Traces of the ink were still left in the paper and modern scientists can use UV light to look through the layers and detect the original texts. Differing versions of the ancient texts have been found in this way. The access to what some may call the "original" Bible is still growing.

What is thought to be the oldest and most reliable near-complete transcribed copy of the New Testament in existence is contained in a Bible that dates to the fourth century (most pages of which are kept at the *British Library)*. The Codex Sinaiticus was obtained from a monastery in Sanai. Interestingly, it has two books not in our modern New Testament, the Epistle of Barnabas and the Shepherd of Hermas.

The latter, also known as "Shepherd" is thought to have been written in about the second century and is said to have been regarded as scripture by an impressive list of early church fathers including Irenaeus, Clement of Alexandria, Tertullian, and Origen.[13]

Also in the *British Library*, the early fifth-century version of the Bible, Codex Alexandrinus, in which the New Testament also includes the books Clement I and Clement II. All of these four books are unheard of in our modern Bibles. Both of these earliest versions of the Bible were found in Egypt where apparently most early Christian Bible writing and scholarship was centered. The four additional books were obviously considered to be part of the scripture by the scribes who copied and assembled these codices.

THE SECRET BIBLE AT YOUR THEOLOGY PROFESSOR'S HOUSE

Now comes the matter of the secret Gospels (or *The Coptic Gospels*). These are some of the earliest Gospels and were said to have been barred from canonization and hidden, under the threat of death. There has been great discussion among scholars about this group of long-hidden Coptic Scriptures.

These are 52 codices in all, leather-bound papyrus manuscripts. These writings were said to have been carefully hidden away in a large clay jar so they could escape destruction ordered by those who would cruelly orchestrate the third and fourth-century church doctrine. They join other *Coptic Gospels* that were already known and published.

After the 52 were found in a cave in 1945 near Nag Hammadi, Egypt, they became known as the *"Nag Hammadi Library."* It was discovered the secret texts had probably come from the oldest monastery in Egypt. They are thought to have been hidden after the Bishop of Egypt, Athanasius sought to destroy all manuscripts but the twenty-seven that became the New Testament.[14]

There are the *Gospels of Phillip*, of *Mary*, of *Peter*, and of *Thomas*. There are also among the collection *The Secret Book of John*, *The Secret Book of Paul*, *The Apocalypse of Paul*, *The Letter of Peter to Paul*, and *The Prayer of the Apostle*.

These secret *Coptic Gospels* were written in the years comparatively quickly following Jesus' death and resurrection, at least as early as (if not even earlier than) the Gospels we have come to know. In other words, they have been understood to perhaps be as (or more) contemporary with the earliest church than anything else we have, yet they somehow missed the publishing deadline to get in the Bible.

Bible scholars have lots of disagreement over the meaning of these writings. They have been called everything from heresy to writings that are probably closer to the original teachings of Jesus.

They say, for example, the kingdom of God is not brought on by some external apocryphal event, but by a presence and a state inside us. Just a couple of simple quotes from the *Gospel of Thomas* may give some idea of why these writings may have drawn some fire from early church leaders who were intent on isolating them from the Biblical canon. One is found in the *Gospel of Thomas* 22:

> Jesus said to them, "When you make the two one, and when you make the inside like the outside and the outside like the inside, and the above like the below, and when you make the male and the female one and the same, so that the male not be male nor the female; and when you fashion eyes in the place of an eye, and a hand in place of a hand, and a foot in place of a foot, and a likeness in place of a likeness; then will you enter the kingdom.[15]

(Considering the advances in technology, that sounds strangely like the twenty-first century.)

Another quotation from the Gospel of Thomas–114–seems even more provocative:

> Simon Peter said to him, "Let Mary leave us, for women are not worthy of life." Jesus said, "I myself shall lead her in order to make her male, so that she too may become a living spirit resembling you males. For every woman who will make herself male will enter the kingdom of heaven.[16]

Could this have been a discourse from Jesus that later prompted Paul to supposedly say: "In Christ, there is neither Jew nor Greek, neither slave nor free, nor male and female"? (Galatians 3:28 – KJV)

Here is a quote from Jesus from the book of Thomas:

> If you bring forth what is within you, what you bring forth will save you. If you do not bring forth what is within you, what you

do not bring forth will destroy you. – Jesus Christ (as quoted in the Gospel of Thomas)[17]

So why did these secret Gospels not see the light of day from the end of the first century until 1945? These *Coptic Gospels* hidden for so long had been the subject of huge controversy within the early Christian movement. These earliest Gospels may have represented freedom and inclusiveness that more aggressive church leaders believed would subject Christianity to too much schism and persecution. Just like the naked young man with the little cloth around his waist in the garden with Jesus, it may have raised too many questions and was too hard to explain.

In her book *Beyond Belief: The Secret Gospel of Thomas*, Biblical researcher Elaine Pagels provides explicit detail on how Irenaeus, a Greek Christian, led a movement to determine which Gospels to keep and which to forbid and destroy. This would be the formation of what he referred to as the *"Cannon of Truth."* He claimed to be building on "apostolic tradition."[18]

While fundamentalists may say the activities were all part of the Holy Spirit acting to retain what was true Gospel, the selection may have been the result of self-preservation and arbitrary dictation of doctrine by someone who claimed to know somebody who personally knew "John the Evangelist." Presumably, this was Polycarp who was also from Irenaeus' hometown of Smyrna (what is today İzmir, Turkey), and grew up with both Greek and Christian influence.

Irenaeus' fascinating defense of why there should be no more, and no less than four Gospels had to do with there being four winds and four zones of the earth (not a profundity in theology or today's world of computerized analytical assessment). It was Irenaeus whose writings first named the four Gospels as Matthew, Mark, Luke, and John in about 180-185 CE (almost two centuries after the birth of Christ).[19]

Even this early designation of Gospels didn't recognize them as holy Scripture in a category with the Old Testament. Irenaeus viewed the writings as being a historical record of the words and deeds of Jesus. He considered them like memoirs of the apostles.[20] At this point, they had also been copied and copied some more, often by non-professional scribes.[21]

The intrigue grows when one considers any claims that John actually wrote the Johannine Gospels have been disproven by most modern Bible scholars. Most scholars now agree that John the apostle wrote neither the Johannine Gospels nor the book of Revelations.

The idea of (over a hundred years after Jesus) knowing someone who knew John (therefore being an ultimate authority on what should be in the Bible) is suspect. Further, most modern Bible scholars agree that none of the four gospels were written by the direct disciples of Jesus whose names they bear.[22]

There is a great deal of scholarly consensus that all of the apostles but John were martyred somewhere around the 60s CE. These are claims of someone in 180-185 CE being individually authorized to choose official written Scripture in a totally different language than those who experienced events, and based on direct knowledge and relationship to Jesus. The claims are a bit wonky considering language barriers, lifespans, and constraints of ancient travel and communication.

Floating around the mysterious edge of all of this is the person (or persons) who indeed did write the Johannine and other Gospels. Irenaeus believed that a legitimate Gospel had to have been written by either a true apostle of Jesus or someone who was a close companion of an apostle.[23] Remember, this is somewhere around 180-185 CE.

What is known is that whatever writing Irenaeus or others may have seen had been copied and even changed several times. It was a practice that continued for centuries. New Testament Scholar Bart Ehrman notes of the practice of copying Scripture that the changes were sometimes substantive and on purpose:

we have to admit that in addition to copying Scripture, they were changing Scripture. Sometimes they didn't mean to—they were simply tired, or inattentive, or, on occasion, inept.

At other times, though, they did mean to make changes, as when they wanted the text to emphasize precisely what they themselves believed, for example about the nature of Christ, or about the role of women in the church, or about the wicked character of their Jewish opponents.[24]

We can also note that it wasn't until more than 300 years after the birth of Christ that in Egypt a Bishop named Athanasius sent a letter to his diocese, and there for the first time, suddenly we see he alone listed the 27 books of the New Testament.[25] This is the same Athanasius who threatened death to any who might hide the *Coptic Gospels*.

He was an Egyptian statesman and politician who certainly did not preside over an ecumenical consensus. He refuted and lashed out at a clandestine meeting of bishops in Tyre who were rebelling against him. History suggests that this bishop/politician presiding over The Church in Egypt and Libya and finding himself at times in and out of political exile was the original New Testament Bible decider.

This all leaves questions:

- How many close companions can an apostle have who are writers, and over how many years? Did Irenaeus know who posed as John? Did he know others who forged the writings?
- How appropriate is it to write Scripture posing as an apostle? Is that inspired by the Holy Spirit?
- How do we know the *Coptic Gospels* which appear to have been written quite early, weren't written by apostles or those who knew them? Was there some kind

of a public relations effort to sort of "clean up" the Gospels to make them have wider appeal and clearer conformity to conventional ideas?

- Given all of the writings that were available to him, purporting to be from any number of apostles, by what authority did Bishop Athanasius in Egypt declare he was listing the canonical books of the New Testament?
- Was there favoritism to the works of certain bogus writers? Was Irenaeus idea of "four winds" of the earth that important to the number of Gospels we inherited? Did the Holy Spirit just *inspire* a lot of deception?
- Finally, have the clergy lied about any of this?

WHICH IS YOUR BIBLE AND WHY?

There was an addition and subtraction of "Bible" books as part of the evolution of Scripture as we know it, and as a part of denominational bias. Some of it is even based on there being "four winds and zones."

Christian Churches don't even agree on what books are in the Bible. At the same time, they try to take LGBTQ people to task and ruin their lives over the meaning of a few ancient-language words that are the subject of a great deal of controversial academic discussion and debate.

Most Christians don't even realize that in Jesus' time what is now known as the Old Testament had not even been fully canonized by the Jews. The Hebrews seem to have recognized a much more fluid and realistic view concerning the development of Scripture than modern Christians hold.

Supporting the idea that the Bible is not a direct dictation from God to humankind, Christian Ethicist David Gushee points to the Rabbinical tradition of study of the *Talmud* which generally is not a part of Christian study:

Writing of Jewish theologians Martin Buber and Franz Rosen-
zweig, Paul Mendes-Flohr says: "Their overarching premise was
that the Hebrew Scripture is at root a record of the dialogue
between God and Israel." Not a dictation. A dialogue. The Bible
records the dialogue between God and God's people. It also
records the dialogues among God's people.[26]

The concepts of "the Rapture" and life after death are put
together from a compilation of individual Christian Scriptures. It is
interesting to note that the Torah does not talk of life in a world
after death, but stresses that people will receive reward or punishment in this life for their deeds on earth.[27]

Much of what is taught now in fundamentalist belief about the
rapture seems to have originated from the 1800s and be based on
the idea of a "pre-tribulation rapture" that is said to have been
introduced by a fundamentalist evangelist John Nelson Darby in
about 1820-1830. It was ultimately integrated into a Scriptural
commentary by Cyrus Schofield in the *Schofield Reference Bible.*
(Eastern Orthodox Catholics and some Protestant denominations
do not believe in the rapture.)

Fundamentalists may even argue over how many times Jesus
will come back for the faithful. Some believe Jesus will appear
three different times to call home those who are "saved." Some
even believe Jesus appeared in what is now North America.
There are pre-tribulation, mid-tribulation, and post-tribulation
theories.

There are even suggestions Darby got his rapture theory from
something he learned from being a Freemason and studying
"Cabalism." Despite widespread agreement on Darby's influence,
some argue vehemently that the idea of the idea of a pre-tribulation rapture existed long before Darby.

The bottom line to all of this is that it may be time for church
leaders to stop the sleight of hand concerning the origins of Scripture and the church, show the cards that are under the table, and

come clean about just how unacceptable it is to proof text LGBTQ people out of full church participation.

What has been suggested with evidence from highly respected scholars is that there are no Gospels actually written by any of the direct apostles of Jesus, nor any Scriptural pronouncements from Jesus that condemn same-sex relations.

There is also evidence that any texts that are thought to be such proclamations from Paul are probably not his writing, and generally misrepresent his approach to salvation through grace and his admonitions not to condemn others.

There is also significant evidence to support a claim there were a lot of people who were not apostles and who were having their way with inserting their own mistakes and opinions in the writing and canonization of texts.

All of this does not mean the Bible is not divinely inspired. It simply means the stark reality is that hundreds of various translators, reporters, and recorders brought scores of versions and years of translations and interpretations to influence and impact what the world now has. Even if one believes God is still inspiring people today to interpret Scripture, it may well be in light of what we now know about science and sociology.

Some who have written about LGBTQ and Biblical translation have made quite a lot of a claim that King James (of King James Translation fame) was gay or bisexual. Although there is much controversial evidence in that regard (he did get married and have children), it doesn't matter. What's important is that James (VI of Scotland and I of England) was the son of Mary Queen of Scots. At just over a year old, he had become King of Scotland.

Subsequently as an adult, he was trying to pull England, Scotland, and Ireland together and reign over them all. This included a need for a tolerant or ecumenical association of denominations. His Bible translators were much more influenced by political concerns than they were by any alleged male liaisons on the part of James. Having been born a Catholic and raised a Protestant where those two things made quite a political difference, he was trying to establish himself as a leader in Christian thought. What better way to do it than to oversee a new translation of the entire Bible?

A new translation of the Bible was also seen as bowing to the wishes of some Protestants to avoid the strict Biblical and prayer structures of the Anglican church and introduce political compromise. Gay or straight makes no difference, James was just playing power politics. If his enthusiastic support of Bible endeavors served to quash any rumors (which did exist) about possible male love interests, all the better.

Just the copyright page of this book credits numerous different versions of translations of the Bible we quote. This doesn't mean Scripture is not holy. This means fully human individuals had a hand in passing along to us the account of what happened as they were inspired to write.

It also means that in very real intervention, subsequent generations seeing themselves as equally "inspired" had their way with the writings. The Christian Church may assert it speaks with outright authority on critical matters of faith. Anyone who denies that such declarations by religious leaders are a moving target associated with societal changes is delusional.

A 25-year-old software engineer recently caused a media stir when he created an Artificial Intelligence app that allowed people to "speak to Jesus."[28] With a warning that the conversations should not be relied on as wholly accurate, the app charges 15.99 USD to chat with Jesus.

We tried it. In response to the question of when he would come back to earth, this AI Jesus had an interesting answer: "I do not know if I will return to earth, but I believe that God's love and mercy are always with us."

The developers may not have realized what a controversial figure they were simulating in their AI communicator. There is lots of disagreement over if and when, and under what circumstances Jesus will return to earth. Even AI can't capture the subtleties.

In the context of whose Bible is inerrant, consider survey data that suggests there are over 45,000 Christian denominations/rites worldwide. These are based on various interpretations and under-standings of the Bible. One might ask each of them which one has the inside track on what Scripture says that is "inerrant."[29]

DON'T ASK DON'T TELL

One sad truth is many Bible scholars know all of this Scriptural contradiction and intrigue and just don't tell their parish members for any number of reasons. The fact is, not all who are in the various forms of ministry are what one might call "Bible scholars."

Research by the Center for Study of Global Christianity esti-mates from their surveys that *only about five percent (5%)* are likely to have formal theological training, including undergraduate Bible degrees or master's degrees.[30]

This, of course, may not be important for those who claim to be getting their understanding of Scripture directly from the Holy Spirit. If one were to ask any one of these pastors which one of tens of thousands of Christian denominations has an inerrant Scriptural view based on the guidance of the Spirit, the answer may very well be, "mine."

New Testament scholar Bart Ehrman says many church leaders know the historical truth about Jesus and simply don't share with their church rank and file everything they know:

"From my conversations with former seminarians, I think that many pastors don't want to make waves, or they don't think their congregations are 'ready' to hear what scholars are saying, or they don't think that their congregations want to hear it. So, they don't tell them."[31]

As a result, many church members have little specific knowledge of the basis of their beliefs. Alan Watts' ministry has included seminary and several years as a university chaplain and an Episcopal Priest. From his years as a minister, he concludes:

I discovered that the educated bourgeoisie of the western world is religiously illiterate. This includes many theological students, not only when they begin their studies but also when they finish.

While it's true that some of the basic attitudes of Judaism and Christianity have sunk deeply into the common sense of most western people, it cannot be assumed that even regular church-goers have so much as an elementary grasp of the doctrines they profess.[32]

The historical evidence of New Testament times and how the Bible evolved is rather clear. It has given a great deal of context to Scripture, a context that has been ignored by some denominations.

Quoting specific stand-alone texts disregarding context doesn't prove anything. Our understanding of the relationship of Scripture to certain events in our lives comes from the insight into the personality of God gained from understanding God's dealings with humankind as described in the Bible. It is context, not proof text one should embrace.

One can take a measure of comfort in a 2021 statement affirmed by more than forty theologians at a prestigious Catholic theological research think tank (WICR) that declares:

Biblical research has recently produced ground-breaking findings whose revolutionary potential cannot be overstated. They finally make it possible to confirm that the two key verses in Leviticus—

and more generally the entire Hebrew Bible—do not prohibit much less condemn free and faithful same-sex relationships. And they also allow a similar degree of confidence with regard to all three passages from the apostle Paul.[33]

The next few chapters of this book will address some broadly used proof texts. Included are scholarship and logical observation concerning the original writings, what they may have meant, and how they have been treated since they were told or written. Also included will be some examples of how Scriptural interpretation for LGBTQ people has been done at times with a different set of rules and a completely inequitable application of understanding when compared to others. It is an exploration of not just how, but why the Scripture has been so misused and misrepresented to torture and marginalize LGBTQ people.

Neither established human authority nor scholarly or priestly discernment alone can lead, because, being human, both are trapped in space/time and thereby prevented from a perspective of total understanding. Rather, it is how the message runs back and forth, over and about, the hubs of the network that it is tried and amended and tempered into wisdom and right action for effecting the Father's will. – Phyllis Tickle[34]

3

GENDER BIAS AS A TRADITION

— DEBORAH —

Everybody born on planet earth since 2500 B.C… has believed , whether they were religious or not, that God and men are in an Old Boy's Club together. . . with God as President. And because they are all guys, they have a special understanding.[1] – Sonia Johnson

Any evaluation of Biblical interpretation through history must be done with the acknowledgment that, for the most part, it has been an endeavor of men. The most abused proof text fueled oppression is directed at women.

A view of this phenomenon and of how women were obscured, blocked, and discounted in the development of Christianity and the Bible can help shed some light on the forms of selective understanding used against LGBTQ persons. To this day large portions of the religious zealot "family values" community use Scripture as the basis for subjugating women. Here are some of the texts:

Let the woman learn in silence with all subjection. But I suffer not a woman to teach nor to usurp authority over the man but to be in silence. (I Timothy 2:11-12 – KJV)

Let your women keep silence in the churches; for it is not permitted unto them to speak; but they are commanded to be under obedience as also saith the law. And if they will learn anything let them ask their husbands at home; for it is a shame for women to speak in church. (I Corinthians 14:34-35 – KJV)

But every woman that prayeth or prophesieth with her head uncovered dishonoureth her head: for that is even all one as if she were shaven. (I Corinthians 11:5 – KJV)

For a man indeed ought not to cover his head forasmuch as he is the image and glory of God: but the woman is the glory of the man. For the man is not of the woman; but the woman is of the man. Neither was the man created for the woman; but the woman for the man. (I Corinthians 11: 7-9 – KJV)

Then the crowning claim for any fundamentalist misogynist:

Wives submit yourselves unto your own husbands as unto the Lord. For the husband is the head of the wife even as Christ is the head of the church, and he is the savior of the body. Therefor as the church is subject unto Christ so let the wives be to their own husbands in everything. (Ephesians 5:22-24 – KJV)

That, "in everything" is the real clincher, isn't it? There is no way of knowing how many millions of women have been subjected to mental, physical, economic, and societal abuse as a result of the proof texting of these Scriptures.

A well-established Biblical scholar Eldon Jay Epp has pointed out a belief the Scripture used to silence women was added post-Paul:

And this combination of literary analysis and text-critical assess-ment has moved a sizable group of scholars to view the passage on "silent women" as a later intrusion into 1 Corinthians and most likely one never written by Paul.[2]

Somewhere along the line women were generally given the right to speak in church. The subjugation of women however is still considered "Scriptural" by some. Calling for what it refers to as, "Biblical Submission," one leading "family values" online organi-zation cites the fifth chapter of Ephesians in admonishing women to follow their husband's lead.

Another conservative publication celebrated the installation of United States Supreme Court Justice Barrett with an article enti-tled "How Strong Women Like Amy Coney Barrett Submit to Their Husbands With Joy."[3]

The web is filled with a new wave of "subject to husband" writ-ings urging compliance with the Ephesians command. Sites online call for the "transformation" of the wife's role and preach compli-ance with the "submission" Scriptures. It is, they proclaim, "God's design for marriage." "Biblical marriage" and "Biblical womanhood" have become well-worn memes among believers in inerrancy.

Religious zealots some years ago set their sights on control of the US Supreme Court. LGBTQ people who think their issues have a snowball's chance in Hell with the new Court need only be reminded of the example that Justice Amy Comey Barrett is reported to have spent two years living in the home of People of Praise founder Kevin Ranaghan in the 90s. The religious organization is heavily positioned against gay marriage.[4]

One would think having been a devoted member of such an organization would compel Barrett to recuse herself from consideration of the topic by the court. Being close enough to those beliefs to occupy the home of its seemingly radical founder would seem to indicate more than just a casual involvement in the group. Recently *The Guardian* carried a couple of harsh articles on what is reported to be Ranaghan's understanding of the place of women and children.[5]

Much of religion has seen early Biblical misogyny as a reflection of the times in which the Scriptures were written. Unfortunately, in too many denominations the prejudice continues with proof texting unabated still today. We can cite examples like the denial of the priesthood to women and only a sprinkling of women showing up in academic theological circles. If women ever abandon Christianity in significant numbers, it is dead. That is a growing existential threat.

The suppression of the full ministry of women has carried over to modern times. Citing a Biblical basis, the Southern Baptist Convention has excluded women from full ministry. The doctrine was challenged when the second largest church in the denomination, Saddleback Church, appointed three women ministers.

The SBC expelled Saddleback from membership along with three other churches because of ordination of women pastors. The belief is that the ordination violates the Baptist statement of "Faith and Message" that says only men are qualified by Scripture to be pastor. A hint at politization of the dogma comes from the fact that women had been allowed as pastors in SBC up until the year 2000.

Calling the decision "testosterone vs. doctrine," Dwight McKissick, Senior Pastor of Cornerstone Baptist church in Arlington, Texas is quoted in the Los Angelos Times as saying the decision to oust Saddleback was not about Scripture nor the Faith and Message rules. He is quoted as adding, "It's driven by power, male supremacy; and it stinks in the nostrils of God."[6]

Some of those in opposition to the ordination of women have been echoing conservative political messages that warned of feminization and liberalizing of the church. It was characterized as a slippery slope to more liberal views.

The use of the Bible by fundamentalists to disenfranchise women from the ministry was challenged even as early as 1975 by a Professor of Systematic Theology at the evangelical Fuller Theological Seminary. Paul K. Jewett even chose known women's advocate Virginia R. Mollenkott to write the forward to his innovative book, *Man as Male and Female*. Jewett was very clear about what his studies had found about women in ministry:

> …we conclude that women have full title to the order of Christian ministry as God shall call them. Let those who scruple only consider what it has cost the church not to use the talents of the woman.
>
> Let anyone consult the hymnbook and see what women poets — Fanny Crosby, Charlotte Elliott, Frances Havergale, Christina Rossetti, Anne Steel — have taught the people of God to sing and then ask what it would mean if such women were allowed to move beyond the relative anonymity of the hymnal to the full visibility men have had in the church as evangelists, preachers, and teachers.
>
> And let all who would help them attain such visibility remember that sharing the ministry with women does not mean requiring them to think, speak, and act like men.[7]

The greatest fear of many misogynistic religious leaders is the feminist movement. The response to the movement has been to enter into a re-emphasis on religion and what they consider God's commanded structure as a way to perpetuate the patriarchal status quo. It's the perpetuation of a situation powerfully stated by Sonia Johnson in her book *Going Out of Our Minds: The Metaphysics of Liberation:*

> and all over the world, in every class, every race, every nation, men rule women, always with violence—the rulers are always caught tighter in the teeth of their system, are more bound, less intellectually and spiritually free, than those they oppress, which is the basic paradox of tyranny.[8]

Presenting a paper in support of feminist theology, University of Chicago Divinity School Theologian Ann E. Carr had this to say:

> Women have claimed a home in a tradition and a theology that has not fully claimed them, but has rather systematically denigrated and excluded them, or denied and impeded their autonomy as human beings and as Christians. Small wonder that some feminist scholars ask whether Christianity is not intrinsically patriarchal, and an unhealthy environment for women, and urge a liberating exodus from its oppressive precincts.[9]

Insistence on selective arbitrary Biblical reference to perpetuate oppression is equally damaging to the oppressors as it is to those under their heel. In this scenario, it falls to the oppressed to redeem the oppressor, and modern assertive women have shown a powerful and thoughtful willingness to take on that burden of redemption for men, including their sons and husbands. In the words of Paulo Freire:

As the oppressed fighting to be human take away the oppressors' power to dominate and suppress, they restore to the oppressors the humanity they had lost in the exercise of oppression. It is only the oppressed who by freeing themselves can free their oppressor.[10]

In a very real way then, the women's liberation movement is also a men's liberation movement.

The problem of self-image borne of years of oppression is complicated for LGBTQ individuals by much of religion's language and perception of gender. God is presented repeatedly only in the male image. It is, in fact, the image of an old, white-haired, well-to-do white heterosexual man. It's stressed that we should strive to be in the image of God or of Christ; both are presented as white male images. Both are assumed to be heterosexual.

Many of us as Christians were taught in Sunday School, that Mary was Jesus' "mommy," Joseph was Jesus' "daddy," and God was Jesus' "father." I was also taught that God made Mary have a baby. No distinction was made to indicate this did not make God a father in the heterosexual sense. As a child, we only saw pictures of God and Jesus as being quite white. Of course, the debate rages about whether Jesus was a person of color. He was. Some Christian teachings even go so far as to claim God is the Father and the Holy Spirit is the mother and Jesus is the little boy in a nice white hetero-sexual family portrait.

That would simply make Mary a surrogate (probably not a word some religions would embrace for her). Joseph is just kind of hanging out there somewhere in stepdad land. (Strangely real estate tradition holds his image can be buried upside down in the front yard to help sell a house. Where did that originate?) It is all very sweet and suggestive of a happy family but not a normal family at all.

HOW JUNIA THE APOSTLE WAS ROBBED

One of the most blatant and damaging examples of manipulation of Biblical understanding to promote patriarchy is found in the accounts of the Apostle Junia. One of the original apostles in the earliest days of the church, Junia deserved special recognition by the Apostle Paul:

> Salute Andronicus and Junia my kinsmen and my fellow prisoners who are of note among the apostles who also were in Christ before me." (Romans 16:7 – KJV)

Right up until the eleventh century, leaders and writers of the church had no hesitation about acknowledging that Junia was a woman and that she was recognized as outstanding as one of the apostles. There was little dispute (if any) that Junia was a woman's name and that "of note among" meant she was particularly noted for her work as an apostle. Those who wrote of her in such a way included Origen, John Chrysostom, Jerome, Ambrosiaster, John Damascus, and many more early church contributors.

It wasn't until the eighteen hundreds that some translators began to decide somehow that Junia was a man. To do so they appear to have created a man's name "Junias" that can't be documented as a name anywhere else in the writings of the early Greco-Roman world. In other words, it appears some simply made up a name to cover their suggestion this "Junias" was a man and not a woman.[11]

The toxic effort for masculinization of Church history didn't stop there. Contemporary with the ruse that Junia was a man (1800's), was the advent of the assertion this Junia(s) was not an Apostle at all but just considered "outstanding" by the Apostles.

The earliest of writings strongly declared Junia to be a woman and an outstanding Apostle. Consider however this later translation that is now among us:

> "Greet Andronicus and Junia my kinsmen and my fellow prisoners. They are well known to the apostles, and they were in Christ before me." That is Romans 16:7 as translated by the **English Standard Version**.

Here are some other examples:

> **New American Standard Bible**: "Greet Andronicus and Junia my kinsfolk and my fellow prisoners who are outstanding in the view of the apostles who also were in Christ before me."

> **Amplified Bible**: "Greet Andronicus and Junias my kinsmen and [once] my fellow prisoners who are held in high esteem in the estimation of the apostles and who were [believers] in Christ before me."

Eldon Jay Epp as Harkness Professor of Biblical Literature emeritus and Dean of Humanities and Social Sciences emeritus at Case Western Reserve University has done an exhaustive exegesis and compilation of all of the various translations and views on the subject. In consideration of the myriad of resources original language versions and various efforts at translation he says this:

> Therefore the conclusion to this investigation is simple and straightforward: there was an apostle Junia. For me this conclusion is indisputable though it will not I fear be undisputed—for the "cultural context" of which I spoke earlier remains in many quarters.[12]

The clear fact of the matter is that the Church community has for recent centuries been denied the impacts that could have come from an accurate acknowledgment that there was one of the earliest apostles and particularly outstanding recognized leaders who was a woman. Junia and women everywhere have been robbed of that history by what appears to many to be intentional manipulation of Biblical translation and exegesis to de-feminize apostolic tradition.

THERE ARE MORE WOMEN WHO HAVE BEEN OBSCURED

There is more that needs to be discovered to correct the traditional Biblical and historical understanding of the participation of women in the early church. There is controversy for example, regarding a woman mentioned by John. The second epistle of John (2 John) is addressed "to the elect lady and to her children."(KJV) The New International Version translates this as "lady chosen by God."

In other Scripture, John refers to his converts as "children." One explanation given for the gender reference here in the greeting in 2 John is that he is referring to the church as "elect lady." Elsewhere in the epistle, however, he refers to another woman "the children of your sister send their greetings." Second John, in verse ten also says meetings occur at the elect lady's house. Starting in verse eight he says she has the authority to reject false teachings. The woman is addressed as the leader of the church.

Linguistic and style comparisons of the English translations suggest at least that the woman church leader's name may have been subsequently omitted by early editors. The greeting is like John three, verse one, "To my dear friend Gaius whom I love in the truth." The man is mentioned by name. John also specifically mentions other men by name (not always in a good way). The most telling comparison comes in the closing. To the woman the author writes in Second John:

"I have much to write to you, but I do not want to use paper and ink. Instead, I hope to visit you and talk with you face to face so that our joy may be complete. The children of your sister who is chosen by God send their greetings."

To Gaius in John Three, he writes: "I have much to write to you, but I do not want to do so with pen and ink. I hope to see you soon and we will talk face-to-face. Peace to you. The friends here send their greetings. Greet the friends there by name."

The form indicates both epistles are to specific persons and not one of them is differentially sent to a group of people in a church. Noted Bible scholars Helen Bond and Joan Taylor, in the documentary "Jesus' Female Disciples–The New Evidence" reveal research suggesting that fifty percent or more of the disciples who followed Jesus were women. They quote Scripture indicating the women even provided for all the disciples "from their own resources."

The history of these women as founders of Christianity has been obscured in much the same way as that of Junia. Imagine the value of having both little girls and little boys know from their early church training there were noted woman disciples and apostles engaged in the formation of Christianity. Of course, one could write an entire book on the women of the Old Testament. Let's just say here that most people don't know that a heroic woman named Deborah was once a powerful prophet and the unquestioned military leader of Israel.

Fact is, since the beginning of Christianity thousands of women have been involved in preserving Christianity and in writing, transcribing, and interpreting the Bible. In their book, *Voices Long Silenced: Women Biblical Interpreters Through the Centuries,* Biblical historians Joy Shroeder and Marion Taylor give an over 300-page accounting of centuries of Biblical interpretation by women since the earliest days of the church to present times.

They also provide research showing instances where efforts were made by men to claim authorship, or where works were destroyed because they were originated by women. Shroeder and Taylor set about to write a book that would "restore the works of overlooked or forgotten female Scriptural interpreters and record their names and stories as a part of the history of Biblical interpretation."[13]

They document that, not only were there concerted efforts over the centuries to manipulate Scripture, there was a dedication to protect gender bias in Biblical interpretation. In some instances, works were destroyed, but colleagues in their group of nuns kept and preserved an account of the work their sister had done.

Shroeder and Taylor's research raises the curtain on voices throughout history that were muted by a patriarchal church. There is no way to know how different would be the Scripture that has come to us today had it not been for the often-successful attempts at silencing women's influence on Scriptural retention and meaning.

THE TRANSGENDER POPE

— POPE JOHN ANGLICUS —

This next piece of history we'll explore is a perfect example of how a church can (and does) effectively control a narrative and write its own version of events (in many cases simply writing women out of existence). Despite the fact that details of a woman pope have been seen in paintings, sculptures, and numerous historical accounts (that briefly even included her in a collection of papal busts in Italy's Siena Cathedral), Pope Joan (John Anglicus) is a heavily disputed, but very evident historical figure of the Catholic church. Just as has been the case with the Apostle Junia, men have attempted to write Pope John Anglicus out of existence. If they can hide a pope, they can certainly hide women in Scripture.

The story is simply this: In the ninth century, a young woman is said to have obscured her gender and risen through the ranks of the priesthood. She was selected to be "Pope John." There are numerous historical writings about the existence of this Pope John Anglicus, but all have been denied and discounted by many church historians.

The one account hardest to dismiss is that from Dominican historian Martin of Troppau. As papal confessor and chaplain to six successive popes, he was in a unique position to know the story. He gave the fullest early version of the account in his "*Chronicle of Popes and Emperors.*" Unfortunately, a seventh pope in the life of Troppau dismissed him and probably poisoned him to keep him quiet.

According to accounts, Pope John Anglicus was only pope for a little less than three years. In an official papal procession down the Via di San Giovanni, the secretly pregnant pope had a miscarriage. Lots of people were said to have witnessed it. This Pope John was banished and died soon after. It wasn't until centuries later the church began an organized effort to discount the story. Most images of Pope John Anglicus were removed from view and from history, and there began a concerted effort to discredit the accounts of this pope ever having existed.

Despite denials, certain evidence remains. The church, for

example, instigated a ceremony to check for testicles on a new pope. This even incorporated a Latin phrase that was said to have been uttered by each cardinal as he saw or touched and confirmed the papal candidate's testicular array by saying, "Duos habet et bene pendetes." This loosely translates to something like, "He has two and they hang nicely."

The phrase persisted, along with the marble papal chairs "sedia estercoraria" with a precisely placed hole in the seat to accommodate the confirmation of biological sex by reaching or looking underneath. At least one of those chairs is still in existence and on display.

After almost 800 years of Anglicus being listed as having been a pope, the fact of a female pope was denied by a new papal order. The Holy See had decided it had better come up with a way of checking to make sure any new pope had a good set of testicles and denying there was ever a pope without them.

It is also said to be the case that for centuries popes have consistently and mysteriously avoided traveling on Via di San Giovanni where Pope John Anglicus fell with a miscarriage.[14]

Having proven worthiness of being a pope, and risen through the ranks under what had to be trying circumstances, Pope John Anglicus would be celebrated and honored in a world that was more fair and just.

IS GOD A SHE?

As long As God is male, male is God. - Mary Daly

————

God Is Not a Boy's Name. - Title of a memoir by Lyn Brakeman

Even though the church does not traditionally portray God as a sexual being, the implication is strongly present that God is a male heterosexual. She is traditionally given all the stereotypical, heterosexual male characteristics. This generally and conveniently avoids Biblical feminine references to God.

The whole limiting and oppressive business of gender identity being associated with righteousness is rampant in much of religion. Most of us who have at any point in our lives been a part of churches in mainstream Christianity have been bombarded by male imagery. We have heard of the "Brotherhood of Man and the Fatherhood of God."

This presentation of God is a sadly limiting one. If one is going to believe in God and that God is spirit, God is neither male nor female. God is neither heterosexual nor same-sexual. God is not binary. God is of no race and without age. God is of all races and of all ages.

In what may be one of its most controversial undertakings in recent times, the Church of England has established projects to determine whether it should begin to refer to God in official liturgy using gender-neutral terms. The idea of departure from terms like "he," "him," and "our Father" for God has already begun to stir opposition, with the *Telegraph* quoting one church leader as saying a change would move the doctrine of the church away from being "grounded in Scriptures."[15]

BIBLE REFERENCES TO GOD AS FEMALE

There are many images of God as a feminine being in the Bible. Here are some examples:

> But Zion said The Lord hath forsaken me and my Lord hath forgotten me. Can a woman forget her suckling child that she should not have compassion on the son of her womb? Yea they may forget yet will I not forget thee. (Isaiah 49:14-15 – KJV)

As one whom his mother comforteth so will I comfort you;
and you shall be comforted in Jerusalem. (Isaiah 66:13 – KJV)

Hearken unto me O house of Jacob and all the remnant of
the house of Israel which are borne by me from the belly which
are carried from the womb. (Isaiah 46:3) I will meet them as a
bear that is bereaved of her whelps. (Hosea 13:8 – KJV)

As an eagle stirreth up her nest fluttereth over her young
spreadeth abroad her wings' taketh them beareth them on her
wings: So the Lord alone did lead him. (Deuteronomy
32:11 – KJV)

Even the King James version quoted here found inescapable
references to God in feminine imagery. It's also important to note
in the original language words denoting feminine gender were
sometimes used and this was lost in translation.[16]

In the Preface to the *New Revised Standard Version* of the Bible,
Bruce Metzger wrote on behalf of the Committee of Translators:

During the almost half a century since the publication of the
RSV, many in the churches have become sensitive to the danger
of linguistic sexism arising from the inherent bias of the English
language towards the masculine gender, a bias that in the case of
the Bible has often restricted or obscured the meaning of the
original text.

The mandates from the Division specified that, in references
to men and women, masculine-oriented language should be elim-
inated as far as this can be done without altering passages that
reflect the historical situation of ancient patriarchal culture.[17]

One feminine exposition from ancient Hebrew references to
God that did not get lost in translation is an aspect of God that
shows up in Hebrew religious writings between the Old Testament
and the New Testament. The "Shekinah" was said to be the feminine manifestation of God. It is written as a feminine reference in

old Hebrew. Modern Christian adaptations understand the Shek-inah to be the visible presence of God as it settled over the Hebrew temple.

Sometimes seen as a cloud, a light, or a fire, the "Shekinah Glory of God" is celebrated, while at the same time not being frequently acknowledged in religious practices as representing the divine feminine. It is viewed as such in ancient Hebrew traditions.

The term is not specifically used in the Bible, but it is in other ancient Hebrew writings. Even so, it is embraced by modern evangelical Christians generally without acknowledgment of the divine feminine characteristics it suggests.

GOD IN OUR LANGUAGE

Religion has too frequently been used as a way of keeping women in their subjugated "place." The language has reflected this. Virginia Ramey Mollenkott makes the point dramatically in her book *Speech Silence Action!*:

> In June 1979 the General Synod of the Reformed Church in America voted to ordain women after many years of debate. Having been part of their debate by speaking at Western Seminary and publishing a lengthy article in the Reformed Journal I was astounded to discover on what basis the matter was finally resolved. According to the news report I saw, the resolution hinged on the meaning of the word "persons" in the denomination's Book of Church Order.
>
> Traditionally "persons" had been interpreted as designating males only. Apparently not until 1979 was the category of "personhood" opened up to include females as well! Anybody who needs additional proof that the language issue is not a trivial one ought to ponder that development for a while![18]

At the beginning of 2021, a minister caused a huge stir among conservatives with a prayer at the start of a Congressional session. He ended the prayer with "Amen and Awomen." The occurrence was repeatedly cited by conservative broadcasters and even quoted in the rally leading up to a violent attack on the US Capitol.

Without weighing in on the politics of the outrage, we can say the closing of the prayer tapped a powerful jealousness with which the church tradition of patriarchy is held to be immune to change. This was true even when a minister attempted with one word to make a good-faith public effort to use language for inclusion of women (who by the way have always been the ones who did most of the work to keep churches alive anyway).

Anne E. Carr was a University of Chicago Divinity School Theologian. For more than 50 years, she was a Roman Catholic nun and member of the Sisters of Charity of the Blessed Virgin Mary (BVM). She became a world-renowned and groundbreaking feminist theologian.

While some believe what they consider the "feminization" of God diminishes the image of the deity, Carr believed removing images of patriarchal hierarchy quite expanded the character of the creator:

> The unknown hidden God of mystery is a final way of speaking of the God who is always more than human images and concepts can suggest. Incomprehensible mystery reminds Christians always that they do not really grasp the one to who symbols point, the God who is dimly known as the mystery, source, fountainhead, and matrix of being that surrounds humankind in inexhaustible light.
>
> This God, of whom mystics also speak, resonates in a special way to women today. For how is it that women remain faithful, despite the negative official messages, to the one whom the church exists to proclaim? Women cling to their own experience of the one who is more, who is hidden, unknown, signified in

startling ways in the teachings of Jesus and the parable of his life.[19]

This example from way back in the eighties demonstrates that feminist theologians have not been seeking a feminization of God, but a removal of what is considered a limiting view that betrays the all-enfolding and incomprehensible expanse of a God, unfettered by patriarchal symbolism.

Even those who adhere to the most strict inerrancy guidelines of Biblical interpretation must agree that when Moses asked God (speaking from the burning bush), "Suppose I go to the Israelites and say to them, 'The God of your fathers has sent me to you,' and they ask me, 'What is *his* name?' Then what shall I tell them?"

God, Godself is quoted here as saying, "'I am who I am.' This is what you are to say to the Israelites: 'I am has sent me to you.'" (Exodus 3:13-14 – NIV)

It was not , "I am he who is." According to a *literal* reading of the Bible, "I am" is God's name when making a self-introduction to others.

Text purist may point out that the reference in Exodus later includes the term "Lord." It is a term that is also used in the Bible for humans and not just God. It was the Greeks who decided the Hebrew word "adon" meant "lord." The Hebrew term can also be understood to mean "sovereign," not having to be gender specific at all.

For centuries, Christianity has ignored what one must admit a Scriptural God insisted to Moses God be called, "I am who I am." The "I am" carries all the mysterious, encompassing, and inclusionary symbolism the God of Moses intended, but it is now discarded in a world of controversial pronouns.

If we are allowed to proof text Paul here, we can say he believed that Christ did not see gender:

> There is neither Jew nor Greek there is neither slave nor free
> there is neither male nor female; for you are all one in Christ
> Jesus. (Galatians 3:28 – KJV)

If God is "I am" and Jesus does not see gender, how can Christ see intra-gender sex, gender ambiguity, or gender discrimination? Those who might want to proof text Paul should agree based on any literal translation of this Scripture that condemnation based on gender issues has no place in the church.

If one *insists* on using standalone proof texts, Paul clearly said Christ does not see gender. There is a mismatch of logic when one applies that thinking while at the same time using the "clobber texts" attributed to Paul to torture same-sex couples.

Research by Jay Michaelson suggests churches struggle with LGBTQ issues because many see the embrace of sexual variety as choosing chaos and dissolution of religion:

> Mythic religion will never accept sexual pluralism, because
> sexual pluralism undermines the idea of order, and subverts
> authority. Such chaos looks like the end of religion. And yet, the
> tragic and beautiful truth is that it is really the doorway to a new
> beginning, practically begging to be unlocked. Or broken down,
> by the force of joy or tears.[20]

4

TEN REASONS SODOM WASN'T SODOMY

We have said that certain texts are used to prove God hates and destroys "homosexuals." We have also said these proof text citations ignore the context of the Scripture to which they point. One Bible story frequently abused in this way (and providing one of the finest examples of misuse) is the story of the destruction of the two ancient cities of Sodom and Gomorrah.

This story has become so linked with same-sex relations that today laws prohibiting sex acts between persons of the same sex are referred to as "sodomy laws." That is a discriminatory religious bias built into the laws. Anal sex is known in some circles as "sodomy." This label persists despite being based on flawed Biblical interpretation.

A TALE OF TWO CITIES

Most of us have heard this story of Sodom and Gomorrah but have you ever read it? Have you ever read the preceding chapters to understand the context of the story? The story can be quite revealing when seen in its entirety. Solid Biblical scholarship heralded by scores of theologians supports the belief that Sodom and Gomorrah were destroyed because of cruel inhospitality and that sexuality was not the issue. Let's look at the story.

LOT'S UNCLE SAVED SODOM'S ASS

The scene begins in Genesis 14 when Lot's uncle Abraham rescues the people of Sodom from invading armies who had taken all their wealth and belongings. Sodom had been sacked by outsiders. During that invasion, Lot and many of the other people of the city were carried away into captivity by the attackers. Abraham tracked and defeated the invading armies and returned with Lot and the other captives to Sodom to restore all the Sodomonians and their belongings.

This is quite an important background for understanding the meaning of the story. Did they teach this in your Sunday School? No.

According to Genesis 14:21-24, this was the exchange between Abraham and the king of Sodom:

And the king of Sodom said unto Abram:
Give me the persons and take the goods to thyself. And Abram said to the king of Sodom I have lift up mine hand unto the Lord the most high God the possessor of heaven and earth

that I will not take from a thread even to a shoe latchet and that I will not take anything that is thine lest thou shouldest say I have made Abram rich. (KJV)

Lot's uncle returned everyone and took no reward whatsoever. One would think Sodom should be respectful and appreciative of that, right? The tale then picks up in Genesis 18 when three individuals appear at the home of Abraham who is a gracious host and welcomes them most lavishly. (There is some question as to whether these three visitors were angels. Some see it as an early foreshadowing of the Trinity. It is recorded in Scripture the strangers appeared as three men.) Subsequent Scriptures suggest the three were two angels and God. Abraham's conversations during the visit were with "the Lord." Genesis 18:1-5 provides a thorough account of how one is supposed to treat a stranger. It says of Abraham that he made quite a to do about the visit, saying to his visitors:

> Let a little water I pray you be fetched and wash your feet and rest yourselves under the tree. And I will fetch a morsel of bread; and comfort ye your hearts after that you shall pass on: for therefore are you come to your servant. And they said so do as thou hast said. And Abraham hastened into the tent unto Sarah & said: Make ready quickly three measures of fine meal knead it and make cakes upon the hearth.
>
> And Abraham ran unto the herd and fetched a calf tender and good and gave it unto a young man: and he hastened to dress it.
>
> And he took butter and milk and the calf which he had dressed and set it before them; and he stood by them under the tree: and they did eat. (Genesis 18:1-5 – KJV)

EXPLICIT BIBLICAL EXAMPLES OF HOSPITALITY

This is hospitality example number one of several in the story. God reveals to Abraham through that encounter there is a terrible outcry about the sin in Sodom and Gomorrah and that God has come to see first-hand what is going on there. Not once is there any mention of same-sex concerns.

Why would God not have been able to see firsthand? According to the story, God needed to check it out, but he/she didn't. God didn't even accompany the group into Sodom, so the concept is a little sketchy anyway. Bear in mind no scene with anybody threatening angels has taken place at this point. There is some kind of sin that has seemingly been called to God's attention.

We have no idea what that was about. There is a hint that having been rescued by Lot's uncle, Sodomites had been ungrateful jerks. After learning during the meeting God's plan already at that point was to destroy the cities of Sodom and Gomorrah, Abraham began to bargain with God. "If there are fifty righteous" would God spare the place? 'Yes.'" If there were forty-five, forty, thirty, twenty, and finally ten righteous in Sodom, God agreed it would be spared. Given the fundamentalists' interpretation of this Scripture is one to determine there weren't even ten good heterosexuals in that town? That was some gay resort.

Next, after some travel, and standing with Abraham and the other two individuals viewing Sodom from afar on a hillside, God leaves, presumably back to Heaven (we guess). Abraham goes home. Two of the three individuals who had been at Abraham's dinner party go on down to Sodom for a little test of the hospitality of the townsfolk.

Lot finds them at the gate and takes them to his house where they are given another dinner party. Again, there is a thorough explanation in the Scripture (almost painfully detailed) of how one is to treat a visitor.

This is lesson number two on hospitality to strangers. During the evening the house is surrounded by all the people of Sodom who inquire about the strangers and demand, "Send them out that we may know them." This is where the Biblical scholarship gets screwy. Centuries of deadly hatred of "homosexuals" have been based on what "know" means here.

Lot offers his two virgin daughters to the crowd to do with as they wish if they will just leave the visitors alone. What a guy right? He is a powerful ancient example of a man's willingness to sacrifice women. The offer is rejected by the crowd.

The crowd insists on seeing these strangers who have come to town. Then they turn on Lot and threaten him. (This is the same Lot, remember, whose uncle had saved the whole town from exile.) The angels pull Lot back in the door and strike the people in the crowd blind.

The angels tell Lot to get his family out of town. He eventually leaves along with his immediate family. On the way out of town, Lot's spouse turns to look at the cities that are being destroyed by fire and she is turned into a pillar of salt. Lot and his daughters escape to a nearby place called Zoar. They subsequently don't feel comfortable there and move into a cave.

TEN WAYS THE OLD "SODOMY" THEORY DOESN'T HOLD WATER

There are at least ten important observations concerning the story of Sodom and Gomorrah that serve to question the theory that the two cities were destroyed because of homosexuality:

1. Since God is omniscient (knows everything) and since God in Genesis 18: 20-32 had discussed the destruction of Sodom with Abraham, God knew cities would be destroyed all along. There is no mention, in God's discussion with Abraham concerning Sodom's destruction, suggesting anything that would indicate homosexuality as the cause.

2. According to Genesis 19:4 Lot's house was surrounded by "all of the people of Sodom without exception" (JB). Is one then to paint them all with the same sexuality brush? There is nothing in Scripture that claims all of the people of Sodom and Gomorrah were homosexual. The fact there were "young and old" would indicate that someone must have been engaging in heterosexual acts somewhere to produce the young.

3. Lot offered his virgin daughters to appease the mob outside his house. If Lot knew the mob to be made up of homosexual men why would Lot offer women to appease them?

4. The Hebrew verb (said to translate English as "to know") purported to be used in Genesis 19: 5 when the people of Sodom say of the angels in Lot's house "bring them out to us that we may know them," does not give us a clear understanding of intent.

The Hebrew verb "*yadha*" is used some 943 times in the Old Testament. Only 10 times out of 943 does it refer to "know" as sexual intercourse, and then it refers to intimate relations between man and wife. There is no suggestion anywhere it might refer to homosexual rape.[1]

It's also important to point out the subjectivity of the long-standing argument of exactly what the Hebrew term for "know" meant. In their book, *The Bible A History the Making and Impact of the Bible,* scholars Stephen M. Miller and Robert V. Huber point out there are only 22 letters in the Hebrew alphabet. (In fact, it's not an alphabet at all because all of them are consonants and it is what is known as an abjad.) In this "abjad" most words used as their roots only three consonants, and readers had to use context and other clues to figure out what the vowel sounds for the words were.[2]

We could use an example from English. Suppose there were only consonants. You saw the word "LT" written. Now that could be lit, lot, late, or let, depending on which consonant sound you decided should be assigned. (Obviously, this is used here for a demonstration of the concept, and the actual translation is much more complicated.) You see where context gets important. It has to depend on one's assumption the candle probably cannot be "late."

You could put it all in context and assume if someone LT the candle it would be lit and not late, but absent the proper context it could be a struggle. (Certainly, this is an oversimplification, but a simple demonstration of just the concept.)

IT'S COMPLICATED

This was all so confusing and complicated that somewhere between the sixth and tenth centuries a group of Jewish priests and scribes known as the Masoretes believed it was important to find the various remnants of texts that had at that point been written down in ancient Hebrew and bring them together such that they were accessible and less confusing to more people.

With this in mind, they set about to interpret, clarify, and notate various of the Hebrew texts. In other words, one of the things they did was to add guides to what we would consider "the vowels" were. They incorporated traditional understanding and relayed their understanding of vocalizations and outlier meanings. Their work was the basis for the definitive Hebrew text that is set in place today.

Modern experience with working to translate ancient scrolls gives a hint of the challenge they faced. The leather could become damp and obscure passages. Portions of scrolls might experience rot and edges had to be cut (along with some of the text) to keep the rot from spreading. Those who believe in inerrancy would say God controlled every letter and every entry. It was a very human exercise, and it was an evolution of reconstruction.

One can see the ancient scribes sitting around the dinner table having an animated discussion about what in the world might the term *"know"* means in various original stories. Or maybe they just decided based on their own cultural biases.

Scribes over the centuries have made errors/alterations, and even added subjective interpretations. Now scholars have an intellectual arm-wrestling match or coin-toss over what those original consonants meant by adding somebody's arbitrary vowels, and people are supposed to allow their dignity and even eternal destiny to depend on it.

Now back to our list. Number:

5. It was a common practice of the people of the times to humiliate a male enemy soldier by subjecting him to anal intercourse. It was not intended as an act of sexual gratification so much as an act of humiliation of one heterosexual man by another. This practice of the time that the people would do such a thing to humiliate an enemy would be based on a belief the humiliation would lie in treating the male enemy soldier like a woman. The act placed the enemy on the woman's lower rung of the social ladder.
If the "bring them out to us that we may *know* them" in this passage even were to refer to same-sex rape, it is rape by heterosexual men seeking to humiliate strangers by treating them like women. That is in no way equated with gay sex of modern times. Of course, this is further complicated by any assumption the strangers had any genitals at all, if they were, indeed, angels.
6. God spared Lot and his daughters from the destruction of Sodom. Genesis 19:33-36 goes on to say how the daughters got Lot

drunk and committed incest with him so they could get pregnant by their father. Would God destroy two cities for homosexuality and save these people so they could go right out and commit incest? Did God not know that was what was going to happen?

7. Even though the Scripture says everybody from Sodom was gathered at Lot's door, no specific reference is ever made to the women of Sodom. Where does it say they were lesbian? It is never even implied. What was their sin?

Those who assume the men were destroyed because they wanted to engage in homosexual rape must jump a long way to conclude the women were lesbian. If the cities were destroyed because of homosexuality, did God destroy the women because their husbands and sons were gay?

8. Lot's future sons-in-law who were engaged to marry his daughters were invited by Lot to leave with him before the town was destroyed. They thought he was joking, rejected the idea, and were presumably destroyed with the townsfolk. Were Lot's daughters about to marry a couple of homosexuals?

9. What about Gomorrah (and maybe other towns of the plain as the Scripture described)? To place the blame for the destruction of Sodom and Gomorrah (and maybe other towns) on one incident that took place in Sodom is to make a lot of assumptions about Gomorrah. How can one conclude one incident in Sodom proves Gomorrah was filled with "homosexuals?"

That would be like saying because a rodeo was held once in Ft. Worth everyone in Dallas rides bulls.

10. The Bible speaks several times with clarification of the destruction of Sodom. Isaiah 3:9 indicates that Sodomites knowingly rejected God. Could their sin be as simple as that? Ezekiel 16:49-50 says, Sodom had pride, an overabundance of bread, abundance, and leisure, but they did not help the poor.

This is what Scripture proof texted in the Bible says.

This is carried over into the New Testament where Sodom is

used in a prediction of the fate of cities that reject the disciples. Christ compared the sin of Sodom with the sin of a city of his own time and makes it clear that the sin of Sodom was rejecting God whose acts they knew. Says Jesus to his Disciples:

> "And whosoever shall not receive you nor hear your words when ye depart out of that house or city shake off the dust of your feet. Verily I say unto you It shall be more tolerable for the land of Sodom and Gomorrah in the day of judgment than for that city." (Matthew 10:14-15 – KJV)

That message was a clear rejection of inhospitality.

Another part of the story you probably have never heard is that the angels told Lot to take his wife and daughters and run for the hills so he would not die in the destruction of Sodom. Lot complained he was not agile enough to make it to the hills so he and the angels decided he would just run over to the little neighboring town of Zoar.

If we are to believe the proof texters, we are to think this Zoar was a heterosexual, Straight town, and Lot and his virgin daughters would be safe there. Lot and his daughters didn't fare very well in Zoar either and ended up moving into a cave. This was the cave, of course, where that little incest matter mentioned earlier took place. The bottom line here is the entire, bigoted, centuries-old perception that both Sodom and Gomorrah were destroyed because of homosexuality is based on loose conjecture, questionable proof texting of Scripture, and absolute rejection of the notion that this God as described in the Old Testament was simply angered by humankind when they were inhumane and harsh to each other, and therefore rejected him.

OH, AND THEN THERE'S THE MATTER OF THE METEOR

Although not included here in our list of ten, there is another reason Sodom wasn't Sodomy. The area was simply hit by a meteor. In 2021 scientists concluded from extensive geological and archeological research that evidence suggests a huge airburst from a meteor hit the Jordan Valley in the area of what has been described as Sodom. The area also included Admah and Zeboim that are additionally mentioned in the Bible as experiencing God's wrath.

Rocks that had been instantly turned into diamonds, melted quartz, and other manifestations of a huge nuclear-type explosion were found in the landscape. The chemical and molecular evidence suggests the area was hit by an enormous, exploding meteor. It left that part of the valley abandoned for 300-600 years because of salt deposits. The paper reporting this finding has been published in the prestigious and peer-reviewed *Scientific Reports*:

> an eyewitness description of this 3600-year-old catastrophic event may have been passed down as an oral tradition that eventually became the written biblical account about the destruction of Sodom. There are no known ancient writings or books of the Bible, other than Genesis, that describe what could be construed as the destruction of a city by an airburst/impact event.[3]

The modern scientific discovery that salt deposits and other chemical manifestations of the meteor impact would have left the Jordan Valley uninhabitable for centuries may even find confirmation by referencing the ancient account in Deuteronomy where there is mention of the poisoning of the land.

Their vine comes from the vine of Sodom and from the fields of
Gomorrah. Their grapes are filled with poison, and their clusters
with bitterness (Deuteronomy 32:320–NIV)

It is not unusual even in modern times for superstitious people
to attach some idea of an outpouring of the wrath of God to
natural occurrences, even to the point of coming up with elaborate
estimations of why God was so angry as to cause the destruction.
One can look at those evangelists who took great pains to
pronounce why God caused a hurricane to hit "homosexual-
tolerant New Orleans." There is nothing unusual to imagine here.
A meteor hit the Jordan Valley, and subsequent generations just
explained it in the best way they could with a cultural and religious
bias.

In a society that had little understanding of the cosmos, having
such massive destruction suddenly appear was best understood
when attributed to a god. Coming up with a way of preventing
such a thing by avoiding specific sin could lessen the fear and create
an illusion that such a dramatic holocaust can be prevented and
controlled by human action.

Considering that, subsequent Scripture (including in the New
Testament) sets up and attests that the purported sin of Sodom that
drew destruction was gross inhospitality to strangers. The story
reinforced the ancient Hebrew concept that the kingdom of God is
within, and it is our responsibility to graciously share that kingdom
with the world. It also gave a very easy prescription for preventing
catastrophic mass destruction, "if you be nice to people, you can
just safely go on with your lives."

It is just this simple: a meteor hit the area. Superstitious people
decided it was the act of a god. Searching for a reason the god was
angry, they settled on inhospitality. Being hospitable to strangers
could appease this god. Subsequent generations with religious,
political, and financial agendas to create hate for LGBTQ people
invented the word "sodomy" and twisted the story. That's how we

got where we are today. These subsequent generations who found economic and religious competitive reasons not to be nice to everybody (and even kill thousands) found a way to make it even easier for heterosexuals, just don't have man-on-man sex and a meteor won't hit you. Sweet!

The beauty for heterosexuals of applying the "sodomite" sexual rape understanding to Sodom, is that it gets them totally off the hook on the holiness of hospitality matter. One can do pretty much anything they want to their guests, and it pales in comparison to dragging them out of the house into the street and trying to publicly put a penis in their hinder parts.

5

WHY YOU NEVER HEAR OF GIBEAH

Strangely, the story of Sodom has been used so frequently to allege God's negative judgment of "homosexuals," while the story of Gibeah has been kept so silent by Bible instructors. It's a story none of us remember from children's Bible school. Even though there are some striking similarities to the Sodom story, the Gibeah account gets little exposure.

There is just as much evidence the people of Gibeah were bent on same-sex rape as there is of that being the plan of the people of

Sodom. Sodom has become so identified with same-sex acts that laws against such acts are referred to as "sodomy laws." One never hears of "Gibeahmy." In a more equitable world, if someone hauls another's female guest out into the street and rapes her to death, it would be called "Gibeahmy." Even though the story is right there in Scripture, it's almost as if a conspiracy of silence has fallen on it.

Proof text folks don't like this story because it messes up their anti-LGBTQ meme. Just as in Sodom, the people of the city of Gibeah surround a house and ask that a male guest be sent out so that they may "know" him (The New International version rather bravely translates this as "have sex with" just as it translates the same word in the Sodom story).

The story of Gibeah and the story of Sodom are the same kind of stories written for the same reason. They are in the Bible to demonstrate God's displeasure toward inhospitality. This purpose is much clearer in the story of Gibeah, yet the church has kept Gibeah obscure. Why?

Here is how the story of Gibeah unfolds:

A Levite who lived near Mount Ephraim had been in Bethlehem Judah where he had gone to retrieve his concubine who had run away from his house and was staying at the house of her father. On their way home, the Levite, the woman, and a male servant found themselves still traveling when nightfall approached. Judges 20: 4 takes up the story from there:

> When they were near Jebus the day was almost gone and the servant said to his master 'Please come let us turn aside into this city of the Jebusites and spend the night in it.' However, his master said 'We will not turn aside into the city of foreigners who are not of the Sons of Israel, but we will go on as far as Gibeah.' (KJV)

The story goes on to tell of how the travelers entered the city of Gibeah and sat down in the street with no one initially offering to take them into their house to spend the night. They were finally taken in by a man from the hill country of Ephraim. The Scripture makes the point here that the people of the town were Benjamites. It emphasizes that Benjamites would not offer shelter for this person.

Sarah Milstein is a *Hebrew and Classic Near Eastern Studies,* Religious Studies Professor at the University of British Columbia. She says of the Gibeah story, "with its anonymous characters, direct speech, and folkloric repetition indicates that this unit must be read and interpreted as literature…"

In her paper "The Story of the Concubine at Gibeah: A Satire on King Saul" she presents in great detail evidence that the Gibeah story was designed to appeal to knowing readers of the time who would interpret it with the story of Sodom as an obvious satirical comparison between the Kings Saul and David:

> As scholars have observed the place names in Judges 19–21 line up with known Saul and David reference points. While the places associated with David are depicted in positive or neutral terms, all of those tied to Saul are negative. Thus, the Levite receives great hospitality in Bethlehem of Judah (David's hometown) and refuses to stop in Jebus (= Jerusalem David's future capital)… Thus, the Levite insists on heading to Gibeah (Saul's capital), where the men turn out to be violent rapists, akin to the Sodomites.[1]

Analyzing the texts of both the Sodom and Gibeah stories, Milstein details how the Gibeah story and its outcomes create satire that is positive for David at Saul's expense. The stories about Hebrew hospitality seemed also to have a double meaning when read in the historical context. This points out again why historical and even political context is important in assessing the intentions of those who originated Biblical literature.

Meanwhile back at Gibeah, while the three strangers were in

the home of the Ephraimite the house was surrounded by the people of Gibeah. They demanded the host send his guests into the street. The old man of the house offered his daughter and the traveler's concubine if the people would leave the Levite alone. (Sounds familiar, eh?) Yet in this case, the mob settled for the concubine who was given to the crowd.

The woman was sexually abused all night and stumbled to the doorstep the next day. There she died. The traveler took the news to all of the tribes of Israel. He even cut the woman's body in pieces and sent a piece to each tribe to underscore his point. Would he have done that to indict a bunch of "homosexuals" for the rape of a woman?

So, the story demonstrates the people of Gibeah did not know how to treat a stranger. Just as those offenders in Sodom, they had demanded "Send them out that we may know (*yadha*) them." They were rude and ugly. Were they LGBTQ? Did they intend same-sex rape? (To engage in same-sex rape in that time and cultural setting would not necessarily have meant they were entirely same-sex attracted, but was imposition of a social stigma.)

They did engage in man-on-woman rape and murder. The Levite is quoted later as saying that they had intended to *kill* him, "During the night the men of Gibeah came after me and surrounded the house intending to *kill* me. They raped my concubine and she died." (Judges 20:5–NIV) Note, he didn't say they intended to have sex with him.

The story casts doubt on the standard interpretation of the Sodom encounter.

A WAR WITH "CHOICE MEN"

When the other tribes received word of the incident in Gibeah, they were so enraged they vowed to go to war. Judges 20:15 tells us that among those arming themselves to defend Gibeah were the inhabitants of Gibeah "who were numbered 700 choice men"

(NAS) The passage goes on to say that each one could sling a stone at a hair and not miss. Is the Old Testament referring here to 700 LGBTQ people as "choice men?"

The Book of Judges tells us of how 26,000 men of the tribe of Benjamin came to the defense of their friends at Gibeah. Now, the other tribes of Israel had to attack three times and lost about 40,000 warriors before the tide of battle finally turned in their favor.

Here were "choice men," highly trained soldiers, for whom 26,000 neighbors came to the rescue and they put up quite a fight against overwhelming odds. No wonder there has been such silence concerning the Gibeah story.

It seems that if one applies the same logic for interpreting the Gibeah story that has been applied to the Sodom story, it must be assumed that neither the men of Sodom nor the men of Gibeah were "homosexual," or that the men of Gibeah were "homosexuals" who raped women and were well-trained warriors; "choice men" who were fearless in battle.

That would upset some ideas of stereotypes. For all the financial, geopolitical, and sociological reasons explored in this book, the official Church has found it convenient to just ignore this story of Gibeah. It doesn't fit the desired meme.

The evidence suggests Sodom was among the cities of the plain hit by a devastating meteor and left desolate for 300-400 years. Subsequent generations explained the destruction by blaming it on a vengeful God, angered by people's inhumanity to each other. Gibeah had struggles with neighbors and seems to have survived among legends to make a political point.

6

COMPANY FOR HEBREWS WAS A
BIG DEAL

The stories of Sodom and Gomorrah and of Gibeah are intended
to demonstrate the importance of helping strangers. They show
God and Israel's great dislike for cruel treatment of guests. The
hospitality theme carries over into the New Testament with the
story of the good Samaritan. There is a recurring theme in the
Bible telling us God desires that we respond to divine love and
goodness by loving each other. "If you have done it unto the least
of one of these little ones you have done it unto me, is God's

message. Numerous stories throughout the Bible illustrate this point.

Hospitality was a central part of Hebrew life. The Jews were not unique in this. As residents of the Fertile Crescent, the early Babylonians made hospitality a special virtue. The Canaanites were so concerned with hospitality they subsidized local gods to protect strangers who happened along. It was customary in Egypt to extend aid to needy travelers. It was also traditional in Egypt and Syria to make a covenant with a visitor as they crossed the threshold of one's home by smearing the doorsill with the blood of a freshly killed animal. The traditions continue in some of the areas today. [1]

The importance of hospitality to the Hebrews was evident from the earliest times. There was no more hospitable gesture than offering food and drink to a visitor. One example of such courtesy occurs in the story of Isaac's engagement to Rebekah (Genesis 24). To prevent the choice of a Canaanite wife by his son Abraham dispatched his servant to his old homeland in Mesopotamia. The servant was found by a fellow named Laban at a well watering his camels. Laban addressed him as an honored guest:

Come in oh blessed of God; why do you stand outside? For I have prepared a house and a place for your camels. So the man came into the house; and Laban ungirded the camels and gave him straw and provender for the camels and water to wash his feet and the feet of the men who were with him. The food was set before him to eat. (Genesis 24: 31-33–KJV)

That is the way strangers and travelers were supposed to be treated. [2] Scripture twice in the Sodom story had detailed descriptions of hosts' reception of strangers as guests. Why would the Bible go into such detail on the way Abraham had treated these strangers or the way Lot treated his visitors? Why a description down to the recipe of what they had to eat? It's all there because it is an example of how Hebrew hospitality was supposed to be extended. It is there to make a point.

The Sodom and Gibeah stories are there to make the same point. There is also the blessing for Abraham and Sarah after this meal with the strangers when God tells them Sarah will have a child. That was considered a good outcome because of Abraham's generosity and courtesy. The story is constructed this way to contrast the good outcome of Abraham's treatment of strangers and the bad outcome of the treatment of strangers by the general townspeople in Sodom.

JUST BE NICE TO STRANGERS

The Old Testament states emphatically that strangers are to be treated properly:

> *And a stranger shalt thou not wrong neither shalt thou oppress him.* (Exodus 22: 20–KJV)
>
> *And a stranger shalt thou not oppress for ye know the heart of a stranger seeing ye were strangers in the land of Egypt.* (Exodus 23: 9–KJV)
>
> *The stranger that sojouneth with you shall be unto you as the homeborn among you and thou shalt love him as thyself.* (Leviticus 19: 23–KJV)
>
> *God loveth the stranger in giving him food and raiment. Love ye therefore the stranger.* (Deuteronomy 10: 18-19–KJV)
>
> *Thou shalt not pervert the justice due to the stranger.* (Deuteronomy 24: 17–KJV)[3]

Hebrew commentary carries reference to the law of hospitality and to the Sodom residents breaking that law. The Midrash is a set of Hebrew Rabbinical commentaries based on writings dating back to about 300 B.C. These were finalized about 200 A.D. *The Midrash* contains this concerning Sodom:

The Sodomites because they had been overbearing saying 'Let us cause the law of hospitality to be forgotten in our midst';
  as it is said 'They are forgotten of the foot that passeth by' (Job 28: 4)
were punished by fire as it is said 'Then the Lord caused fire to rain upon Sodom and upon Gomorrah brimstone and fire' etc. (Gen. 19: 24)[4]

Many early Christian writers make it quite clear that breaking the covenant of hospitality was the sin of Sodom. Origen for example had this to say:

Hear this you who close your house to guests! Lot lived among the Sodomites. We do not read of any other deeds of his...he escaped the flames escaped the fire on account of one thing only. He opened his home to guests. The angels entered the hospitable household; the flames entered those homes closed to guests.[5]

Saint Ambrose also saw inhospitality as the reason for the destruction of Sodom saying: "Lot placed the hospitality of his house—sacred even among a barbarous people—above the modesty (of his daughters)."[6] John Cassian as late as the 4th century rejected or ignored a homosexual interpretation of the destruction of Sodom saying it was caused by gluttony.[7]

It's also important to consider the form reflected in the the Sodom and Gibeah stories did not exist in isolation in that part of the world. A lot of cultures had stories emphasizing the gods were inclined to occasionally test persons for their hospitality to strangers.

Even tour guides in Greece to this day may tell the story from Greek tradition of how Zeus was the protector of the traveler. He would occasionally send deities disguised as humble strangers to visit people. There were great rewards or dire consequences in response to how the hosts received their divine guests. This is cited as the basis for wonderful Greek hospitality.

Why would the understanding of the story that is so much

based on a regional tradition of all kinds of Gods be changed by the Church? Why wouldn't the message of hospitality and generosity be more important to the Church than stigmatizing sodomy? How ironic that religions are using a bastardization of the Sodom story to justify inhospitality and the exclusion of LGBTQ+ persons from fellowship. It is in itself a commission of the real sin of Sodom.

For reasons we have discussed in this book, the medieval Christian church decided to sexualize the Sodom story and the outfall has remained with us since. The original and similar stories of Sodom, Gomorrah, and Gibeah were told in a form of regional tradition to emphasize the importance of empathy and hospitality with strangers.

They were also there to deal with any public sense of helplessness at the prospect of being vaporized by some big body that seemed to strike out of nowhere. To prevent such disaster, all one had to do was be gracious to guests, please this very powerful God, and live in relative safety.

The Church changed the stories for its own political and commercial purposes. It is just as simple as that.

7

BLATANT SEXISM - SCIENTIFIC NAIVETÉ

Beware of false knowledge; it is more dangerous than ignorance.
– George Bernard Shaw

The next short chapters will spend a little time establishing some context for the theological assault with weaponized and proof texted Scriptures we will later discuss. With our societal conditioning, it's difficult to understand there was a time when a separate homosexual identity did not exist. It is hard to imagine a culture in which homosexuality is not a socially or ethnically distinct thing except in extreme cases. Just such a condition existed however in Old Testament times.

Yale University Historian John Boswell in his book, *Christianity Social Tolerance, and Homosexuality,* says there wasn't even a common word for same-sex-oriented individuals in Biblical times. He writes this:

In spite of misleading English translations which may imply the contrary, the word "homosexual" does not occur in the Bible: no extant text or manuscript Hebrew, Greek, Syriac, or Aramaic contains such a word. In fact, none of these languages ever contained a word corresponding to the English "homosexual," nor did any languages have such a term before the late nineteenth century. Neither Hebrew nor Arabic has such a word today...[1]

When more recent translations of the Bible insert the word "homosexual" in some texts, we believe it is a reflection of modern-day bias and perhaps an intentional misrepresentation of Scripture. It is reasonable to believe that there was an attitude in Biblical times that simply did not acknowledge male same-sex attraction as a specific orientation. Middle Eastern anthropologists have discovered that sexual contact between males was rampant in Biblical times and those cultures did not regard this with any degree of disapproval.[2]

The structure of ancient society did not lend itself to a separate identity or focused same-sex relationships as modern society knows them. There was no health insurance, no welfare, and no social security. Getting married and having children was almost a necessity for survival. If you did not have children as you grew older, there was no one with any obligation to take care of you.

Most of the same-sex activity of the times would have been between persons who also maintained heterosexual marriages with one goal being to have children. Kids were the social safety nets of the time.

There is evidence one group known as "catamites" was singled out. They were extremely effeminate men who played a woman's role. They were openly and exclusively same-sexually active and advertised themselves as being so. There is a strong indication they were looked down on by their societies, not because they were "homosexuals" but because they were acting like women.[3] Women were not greatly respected in those cultures. Any male who would give up his "maleness" and all the privilege it brought must have been looked upon as a fool.

A Wijngaard Institute for Catholic Research statement on same-sex relationships speaks quite clearly about interpreting the Bible based on an understanding of the sexuality of the times:

> For ethics as for anthropology, the lack of knowledge about sexual identity is an obvious problem: one cannot conclude an exact ethical evaluation of acts of a sexual nature without an adequate understanding of the sexual nature of the subject of the acts themselves (agitur sequitur esse).
>
> Biblical texts were based on a knowledge of sexuality specific to their time and they need to be read on the basis of the greater knowledge we have today.[4]

YOU DON'T NEED TO WASTE THAT SEED

One important thing to keep in mind when one talks about ancient Hebrew concepts of sexuality is that they misunderstood the basic facts of life. They did not know of the necessary roles played by both the female egg and the male sperm in reproduction.

It was thought the reproductive elements were all contained in the seed of the man. The belief was that this "seed" simply grew when planted in the body of a female into a child.[5] (It was not until 1854 that science confirmed both an egg and a sperm were necessary for conception. In that year a frog egg and sperm were observed in the act of fertilization under a microscope.[6]) Eureka!

OH ONAN! OH MY!

So important was the protection and preservation of the male seed in Israelite culture that Genesis (38: 8-10) tells the story of Onan who spilled his seed on the ground in an act of disobedience and so displeased God by that action God struck him dead. Because of that Old Testament story, masturbation was to become known in some religious circles as "Onanism."

Poor Onan! Not only did God strike him dead, but he has had to go through all of history since that time known only as the world's most famous wanker.

The misperception that the male seed was planted in a woman and grew into a baby like a kernel of wheat grows into a stalk was terribly degrading to women. As time passed an almost ceremonial aura grew around this arrogant attitude toward the male seed. Writing in New Testament times, Philo Judaeus, an Alexandrian Jew, gives us some insight into how these attitudes were still applied in his time, and how they objectified women. He wrote:

> And there are particular periods affecting the health of a woman when a man may not touch her but during that time, he must abstain from all connection with her, respecting the laws of nature.
>
> And at the same time, he must learn not to waste his vigor in the pursuit of an unseemly and barbarous pleasure; for such conduct would be like that of a husbandman who out of drunkenness or sudden insanity should sow wheat or barley in lakes or flooded torrents instead of over the fertile plains; for it is proper to cast seed upon fields when they are dry in order that it may bear abundant fruit.[7]

Philo calls a man who would knowingly plant his seed in a barren woman "...an enemy of God and an enemy of nature." He compares such an act with the sex lives of pigs and goats. Remember, this is not homosexuality, this is having intercourse with a woman who can't bear a child.[8]

DO LESBIANS GET A PASS?

The attitude toward "wasting of the male seed" carried over into Christian tradition. Because the male "seed" was thought to contain the whole of human offspring, dogmatic Christian tradition has long considered male masturbation comparable to abortion.[9] Even today in the Catholic church it is thought masturbation can lead one to mortal sin.

The attitude toward the male seed persisted even after biological discoveries disproved the premise.

The perception of the importance of the male "seed" and failure to recognize the woman's part in the family lineage is popularly thought to account for the fact there are no prohibitions of lesbian activities in the Bible. Because they carried no "seed" it was deemed unimportant if women sexually stimulated each other. The discussion of lesbianism in Rabbinical literature does give us some interesting insight into the distinctions made between female and male same-sex activities in Hebrew culture.

The Talmud extended the prohibition of male homosexuality to the female— but not the penalty. It was not considered a specific sexual sin for the female as it was for the male. It was considered rather a general religious sin. The conclusion was that since there was in lesbianism no genital intercourse and no wasting of seed it would not be considered a perversion of God's intent. The lesbian was not to be punished as the male same-sex perpetrator would be and she would be "permitted" to marry a priest[10] (something maybe worse than death for your average lesbian).

The two primary reasons for a negative reaction to male same-sex relationships during Old Testament times were that the male seed was "wasted" and that men were somehow lowering themselves to play a woman's role. The first reason was based on blatant biological ignorance and the second on ungodly sexism.

8

THE BIG SENSATION OF ABOMINATION?

It is good for us to ask ourselves if we still live in the period in which we need the Law, or if instead we are fully aware of having received the grace of becoming children of God so as to live in love. – Pope Francis[1]

Thou shalt not lie with mankind as with womankind: it is abomination. (Leviticus 18: 22 – KJV)

This is one of the most cited Scriptures people haul out while declaring opposition to LGBTQ relationships. Let's point out here this is probably the Scriptural reference in which the greatest hypocrisy of those who hurl the citation becomes apparent. What in the world could compel a preacher to hang around a house financed with a loan at interest and eat bacon for breakfast while using Leviticus to condemn LGBTQ people to Hell? There is a high probability most folks who cite this Scripture are guilty of one or more of the Levitical law transgressions referred to as "abomination" or "unclean."

There is a scene in the HBO drama *The West Wing* that poignantly highlights the hypocrisy in proof texting the Old Testament to condemn individuals today. To set the stage, we see the character playing the president of the U.S. being questioned by a visiting fundamentalist who points to Leviticus 18:22 in condemnation of LGBTQ people. In the script, writer Aaron Sorkin gives the President a masterful response:

> I wanted to ask you a couple of questions while I have you here. I'm interested in selling my youngest daughter into slavery as sanctioned in Exodus 21:7. She's a Georgetown sophomore, speaks fluent Italian, always cleared the table when it was her turn. What would a good price for her be?[2]

He went on in the show to point out the absurdity of citing Leviticus for punishing people for working on the Sabbath, planting more than one kind of crop in a field, wearing garments with more than one kind of thread, or football players touching the skin of a dead pig.

We use the quote because it so clearly captures the quandary of trying to proof text Leviticus.

The matter of "abomination" is a clear reference to idol worship. In the book of Leviticus, the word "abomination" is translated from the Hebrew word *toevah*. In Hebrew, the word *toevah* (or *toebah*) often specifically refers to idol worship.[3]

Historian Boswell suggested the Hebrew word "*toevah*" which has been translated as "abomination" should be taken to suggest being "unclean like Gentiles," associated with "ethnic contamination" and idolatry. It would be considered "unclean" as associated with heathens and their idols, therefore challenging the need to distinguish Hebrew culture and religion.[4]

Consider a Gentile trying to hold onto and impose ancient Levitical laws on others, while just being a Gentile makes them unclean (*toevah*) under those same laws. Protestants would, under their own translation, be an "abomination."

Considering the history of these writings, that the Canaanite culture included fertility rites that were various types of sexual intercourse in the temples, any identification with those rites was considered disgusting to God. According to respected Biblical linguists, theologians, and historians, *toevah* can be interpreted as something that was displeasing to God because it had to do with idols. It was also something that posed a threat to the maintaining of the status of the Israelite priests and religious institutions.

It's necessary to remember that in most cases those who invoke the Levitical prohibitions concerning homosexuality are those who refuse to recognize as applicable other sanctions against activities associated by the Levitical priests as something unclean before God. Most of them say that many other rules which also appear in Leviticus and have to do with the concept of clean and unclean must be interpreted in the light of the time and the context in which they were made. These include rules against these things that are considered "unclean:"

- Planting two kinds of seed in one field
- Eating meat with blood in it
- Being tattooed
- Wearing clothes with mixed yarn material
- Crossbreeding livestock
- Loaning money at interest
- Cutting a man's hair
- Clipping beards
- Eating rabbit or pork
- Eating shrimp, lobster, oysters, crabs, or clams
- Being nude even in front of a family member
- Touching a woman during menses

- Touching items touched by women during menses

Male same-sex relations as part of idol worship were seen as being somehow outside the Hebrew concept of an "ideal" creation, but then again, so was being a non-Hebrew. (even what we would now call "Christian," by the way).

Same-sex relations were undoubtedly only visible in the context of male prostitution for a competing god to Yahweh, peddrasty, or adultry, or all of the above. This would not only be "seed spilling" but idol worship. Those who cite Levitical law in the condemnation of LGBTQ persons fail to apply it to themselves.

If they did, all indigenous persons who have been displaced in the world would have their land back. For this claim, we can proof text Leviticus chapter twenty-five. Isn't it strange that a book of the Bible that has been used to bring such oppression to LGBTQ people also includes an incredible proclamation of liberty and restoration?

> on the Day of Atonement sound the trumpet throughout your land. Consecrate the fiftieth year and proclaim liberty throughout the land to all its inhabitants. It shall be a jubilee for you; each of you is to return to your family property and to your own clan. (Leviticus 25: 9-10–KJV)

This is the proclamation of the *Year of Jubilee*! Each 50th year in Israel was a year in which property was to be restored to its original owner and slaves and prisoners were to be set free. In a term that would stir modern Right-wing fears of conspiracy, we can say it was God's "Great Reset." No one generally sees fundamentalist conservatives ever designating a year when they are going to clean out the prisons or forgive all debt and real estate losses.

A BIBLE TRADITIONALISTS' REAL ESTATE MESS

If we are going to strictly apply the rules of the Old Testament, we must recognize that under the rules of Jubilee there were also very restrictive laws regarding buying and selling. They are laws that would also shut down our system of commerce. Now imagine the chaos these next verses would bring to a modern society that held strongly to abiding by the laws in Leviticus:

> The land shall not be sold forever: for the land is mine for ye are strangers and sojourners with me. And in all the land of your possession ye shall grant a redemption for the land. If thy brother be waxen poor and hath sold away some of his possession and if any of his kin come to redeem it then shall he redeem that which his brother sold.
>
> And if the man have none to redeem it and himself be able to redeem it; Then let him count the years of the sale thereof and restore the overplus unto the man to whom he sold it; that he may return unto his possession.
>
> But if he be not able to restore it to him then that which is sold shall remain in the hand of him that hath bought it until the year of Jubilee: and in the jubilee it shall go out and he shall return unto his possession. (Leviticus 25:23-28–KJV)

If you have any real estate or lawyer friends this would drive them crazy. The verses go on to dictate laws about buying and selling that would put our stock market, banks, and real estate companies out of business. There simply is not even the slightest inclination in even the most radical fundamentalist churches to suggest anyone needs to abide by these rules. Why? (Perhaps, if we are going to operate under Biblical laws, anyone who owes money to a fundamentalist should demand a legal amendment to the loan papers spelling out the exact date for Jubilee, and the expectation the loan be expunged at that time.)

Jubilee required debts be canceled and land be returned. If one is going to take a fundamentalist approach to Scripture, this must be honored. In earlier Christianity, a pope (Bonafice VIII) established "The Holy Year of Jubilee" for the Roman Christian Church. For years, the faithful were given special indulgences and prizes for making a pilgrimage to Rome during "Jubilee." True fundamentalism requires canceling debt and restoring land to the indigenous in a designated Jubilee year. (Let's do it Global Methodists!)

Not surprisingly, that very specific and drastic Levitical demand for Jubilee evolved into ultimately giving people a medal for making a trip to Rome. Now "Jubilee" is more like, rattling a tambourine and singing some praise choruses. It is, leave the land, leave the debt, leave the prisoners and institute our own arbitrary application of Old Testament Law involving a team of praise leaders and a smoke machine.

Many fundamentalist preachers who rail against LGBTQ with Levitical law are probably standing in a church financed with interest-bearing loans. (Loaning money with interest, of course, is a violation of Biblical law.) Yet LGBTQ people must deal with straining over every little original word of translation and nuance to defend against hugely destructive assaults on freedoms using references to Levitical laws.

It's disgusting to have to spell out all these theological explanations over and over. It remains necessary only because of the massive fraud undertaken by those in various churches to try to make LGBTQ people all believe we are somehow special where strict interpretation and righteous Godly judgment referencing Leviticus is concerned. This rampant, bold, in-your-face hypocrisy is just passed over with abandon.

Again, the question is not so much whether the Bible condemns LGBTQ people, as it is why they are singled out for special damning and selective imposition of guilt from proof texters.

WHICH LEVITICUS?

Old Testament Biblical researcher and scholar Idan Dershowitz is Chair of Hebrew Bible and Its Exegesis at the University of Potsdam. He has uncovered evidence suggesting an earlier version of the laws in Leviticus accepted sex between men.

Evidence also indicates the original texts had to do with incest and may have been changed by a later editor who opposed same-sex intercourse. Dershowitz makes the argument that earlier versions of Leviticus not only lacked an explicit blanket prohibition against male same-sex relations but that the texts even reflected acceptance of typical male same-sex couplings.[5]

He even explores other Near East writings contemporary with the time when the Priestly scribe(s) may have altered the original text as a way of changing quiet acceptance to a prohibition of male same-sex practices. Dershowitz has sought to determine the nature of those other cultural and intellectual influences.[6]

Still, it doesn't matter. The rules for the canonization of Scripture are such that Moses could walk down Mt. Sinai right now with a new set of tablets and the Bible would not change. The rules made up by somebody somewhere set it all in stone no matter how strangely or questionably it all came to be. The only things that can change are our interpretation and understanding and our appreciation for the fact that the sourcing is always a little suspect.

We have pointed out one publication that has over 900 pages just listing all of the English language translation versions of the Bible. It's also true not all Christian denominations even agree on what books should be included in the Bible. Unfortunately, no amount of work to shed light on interpretation seems to make a difference to many Christians.

When it is all boiled down, the proof texters fall back on a "preponderance of evidence" kind of argument that suggests God just generally detests homosexuality and all Scripture should be considered with that in mind.

They propose that same-sexuality is unnatural, nasty, and a disruption of the natural order of things. Those are all prejudicial opinions and not facts. The real argument they are making is God feels exactly like they do, therefore the way they read Scripture is how God meant it to be understood.

Except for just having been considered "unclean" during certain times of their life and the year, lesbians pretty much escape some of the aspects of sin preached by purveyors of Levitical condemnation. In these Scriptures, there is no mention of any thought that a woman should not lie with a woman as with a man. Somehow that thought was inconsequential to the Hebrew creation ideal.

It was in the Hebrew perception of the compromising of the male by placing him in what they considered the lower role of a female the Hebrews found their concept of creational idealism threatened. The act was therefore considered "unclean."

In other words, a part of their perception of the ideal creation was blatant sexism and patriarchal arrogance. Just because the Bible reveals to us the Levitical priests were scientifically ignorant, arrogant misogynist patriarchs does not mean God wants us to be like them, nor let their ancient pronouncements rule our lives.

HOW CLEAN IS "CLEAN?"

In Acts 10:9-16 can be found the story of Simon Peter's vision in which God shows him all kinds of creatures considered unclean under the law and told him to "take and eat." It is these Levitical laws that had designated those creatures unclean. What then can be concluded about Simon Peter's vision? Was God telling Simon Peter to sin?

So what did "unclean" mean? There is no English word that corresponds with the Hebrew concept of the term we attempt to translate as "unclean." We might need to stretch our imagination to try to grasp this concept. The word in ancient Hebrew did not have a single unchangeable meaning. It expressed an emotion or feeling about things rather than a logical reality.

Even the distinction between "clean," "unclean," and "holy" was not well defined. For example, some Scripture was so holy as to "defile the hands" and in order not to be unclean persons had to wash their hands after they touched it. The bearing of children was considered to render a person unclean even though that practice was encouraged and certainly not sinful. How can we hope to understand a culture in which both the sacred and sinful defile and both innocent and sinful conditions are *tamé* or unclean?

The Hebrew concept we have come to understand as meaning both "clean" and "unclean" extended to the categorization of things in nature by a strange measurement of their "cleanness" based on how closely they resembled the ancient Jewish understanding of the ideal creation.

OF PIGS COWS AND CRUSTACEANS

This ancient Hebrew law in Leviticus then prohibited persons from eating anything that came from the water and did not have fins and scales. This entire concept implies anything that lives in the water and does not have fins and scales exists somehow contrary to God's ideal (this, despite a claim God made it all). To this way of thinking the ideal land animal must have cloven hooves and chew a cud.

That meant a cow would fit the concept of some kind of perfection in God's creation, but a horse or pig would be considered somehow imperfect. They were kind of the creator's factory seconds. Such a concept would seem contrary to any belief in the beauty and importance of all God's creatures. The ancients also had no way of taking into account the interdependence of all the creatures in the environment and the ecological balance that provides.

Even the most avid fundamentalists have among themselves a kind of unspoken agreement to overlook some of the prohibitions in the Levitical laws as outdated concepts. That is their brand of selective "inerrancy."

THE DIRTY NINE-TOE WONDER

The concept of "unclean" was particularly harsh as it was applied to people. Anyone who had a flaw was considered unclean. If a person had lost a toe or was born with only nine toes for example that person would be considered not whole and therefore unclean. That person's presence in the temple would be considered to defile the temple. The very appearance of our nine-toed friend in church would be unclean before God by its very nature. He/She would be a nine-toed insult unto the Lord. God forbid a nine-toed woman ever walk into a tabernacle!

The presence of a barren woman or a blind or deaf person would defile the temple. A woman was considered "unclean" during her menstrual period, her presence defiling. Even anything she touched was considered "unclean." The presence of any woman would defile certain parts of the temple.

Few modern-day priests or ministers would turn a person away from communion for violating any of those concepts of "cleanliness" today. Can you imagine a Catholic priest making you let him count your toes before he gave you communion? Some however point to Levitical prohibitions in turning away LGBTQ persons. They will point to their own version of the "natural order of things." You may notice it's quite arbitrary and selective.

To help understand all of this consider radical Islam cultures like the Taliban which is said not to believe in people listening to recorded music. It is considered a bad influence. It's associated with the heathen. That doesn't mean most of us will feel guilty or be swept with overpowering shame when we listen to music. God may not strike dead all the rock bands.

In 2021, in fact, a Taliban spokesman for "Vice and Virtue" enforcement said Afghanistan would have to restore the act of cutting off hands as being necessary for security. No government should feel guilty for not following that lead.

At the same time just because some Mennonites ride around in horse-drawn wagons in deference to their religion doesn't mean I'm going to abandon or feel guilty before the Lord driving my nice automobile. I can say to that person "more power to you and your horse you rode in on" and I can drive away totally guilt-free.

There are fundamentalist Christian cults that still believe women should not show their ankles, wear makeup, or go with their heads uncovered. All other women in society are probably not cowering in shame, being tossed out by families, or losing friends or jobs because they wear short dresses, sport nice hairdos, and wear makeup.

What is the difference between these prohibitions and the constant societal reference to Leviticus where LGBTQ is involved? None! It is looking at a demand for simply embracing or rejecting the dogmatic proscriptions of a religious sect regarding what is considered unholy and sinful. It's just as simple as that and just as ridiculous.

Nevertheless, this book continues with help for those who must defend against the onslaught of this type of political and cultural theology.

FLAWED AND IGNORANT ANCIENT CONCEPTS SHOULD NOT PREVAIL

Ancients simply misunderstood reproduction. They believed the male seed grew into a child after being planted in a woman. The idea was that any seed was destined to be so planted and that any other distribution of the seed was a waste. Since the seed was thought to contain the child, any waste could be equated with murder. They had no way of knowing about the microscopic understanding of sperm. They had no way of knowing that even under what they would have considered ideal conditions only one sperm might have a chance to survive and grow into a child. Even when practicing "clean" intercourse, when one of those little sperm survived to fertilize an egg about 80 million other sperm died in the process.

They also had no way of knowing the seed didn't just sit there in the body waiting to be planted. That's because they were scientifically ignorant. In a biologically healthy male sperm are constantly being produced. Those not emitted are simply killed and absorbed by the body and replaced by new ones. The whole idea the seed might be wasted is simply not valid. So, one can say the Levitical prohibition of male-male sexual activity was based on:

- A response to such practices as they related to idol worship
- An ancient Jewish conception of the ideal in creation
- An ignorant belief that the male seed was wasted if it did not grow into a child

Today:

- There is no reason for us to equate same-sex practices with idol worship.
- Modern science has taught us we must respect all of nature as important and interdependent.
- The male seed does not just sit and wait to be planted and is constantly healthily reproduced therefore cannot be wasted.
- If we recognize the fact men and women are equal there can be nothing wrong with a man being "treated like a woman" (or even treated as a woman).
- Science has changed the concepts of disease and cooking such that it is safe to eat pork and other meats.
- Old superstitions about disease and evil "clean and unclean" have been replaced by an understanding of

how germs and worms cause disease, resulting in more
reliable concepts of cleanliness.

Why have so many of us allowed ourselves to be intimidated by
persons who single out LGBTQ and decide one passage of
Leviticus is terribly relevant and important today while they admit
most of the rest of it probably should not be taken too literally in
our time?

9

LIFE WITH THE NASTY CANAANITES

Religious responses to political expediencies are evident throughout history. As we look at the Old Testament references to sex between persons of the same sex, it's important to know the Hebrews frequently found themselves making rules and decisions in response to foreign influences. Anyone who has seen the movie "The Ten Commandments," or read the Old Testament knows a little about the period of slavery in Egypt and the subsequent exodus of the Hebrews from that country.

The Bible says after many years of wandering in the wilderness the Hebrews finally settled in what they understood to be God's promised land. It was occupied by several different nations and was known to the Israelites as the land of "Canaan."

WHEN IN CANAAN

A reading of the book of Joshua might lead one to believe Israel swept into Canaan, destroyed all its inhabitants, and took their place in the land. The book of Judges tells it differently. That is a story of some tribes destroying all the occupants of territories they had staked out while others moved in side-by-side with the Canaanites.

Judges is probably more detailed and reflective of what happened. There is a great deal of evidence in the Old Testament of Israel's attraction to the Canaanite culture. There is evidence this even extends to influences on the royal ideology of the Davidic Kingdom and to Jerusalem theology through the traditions of the Jebusites.[1]

HEY, THE KIDS, ARE DOING CANAANITE STUFF

In Canaan, the Hebrews were faced with an enormous cultural challenge. They began to assimilate into the relatively sophisticated Canaanite culture. This society was based on agriculture and had established cities and customs. The young people of Israel began to be absorbed by Canaanite society.[2] There was a threat the Israelite culture might disappear. Little is said, for example, about the early Israelite practice of child sacrifice. Numerous verses in the Bible address a problem with some of the children of Israel allowing their children to be "passed through the fire" of child sacrifice to appease foreign gods.

The priests of Israel became concerned with the need to guard their traditions against heathen intrusion. In response to that challenge, Hebrew priests composed the Levitical laws.

One great concern was the sexual practices of the Canaanites. They were deeply interwoven with idol worship. Sex was elevated to the realm of the divine. The Baal worshipers believed gods' powers were disclosed through fertility. Their gods were sexual and were worshiped in sexual rites. The purpose of religion was to keep the gods' cycle of fertility at a fever pitch so humankind would have plenty of crop's, livestock, and children.[3]

The religion of this culture recognized a cyclical struggle between Baal who represented fertility and Mot (Death) who represented infertility. As representations of Baal "pillars" were constructed. Asherah was a fertility goddess. She was represented by a figure of a fruitful tree.[4]

In some ancient cultures the king and queen of a land engaged in the sex act as representatives of the gods. In the Canaanite culture however, this role may have extended to all of the people. The ritualistic involvement of sex with theology and religious practices reportedly didn't detract from the celebration of sex in the everyday lives of the Canaanites.[5]

The children of Israel related their own God Yahweh to fertility: It was Yahweh who established the regular course of the seasons with seedtime and harvest as times of paramount importance (Genesis 8: 22). It was Yahweh who caused droughts as punishment on the people because of the actions of kings (2 Samuel 21; 1 Kings 17). Indeed, Yahweh was the God who received the offering of first fruits of the harvest presumably because the deity who fertilized the ground was its proper owner (Deuteronomy 26).

Yahweh is likewise involved in the conception and birth of humans.[6] God is pictured in the Bible as closing wombs to bring infertility and as opening wombs, even of very old persons, as the giver of fertility in humankind. Some Israelites began to believe fertility rites even to the point of cult prostitution should be a part of the worship of Yahweh. One can see how lines between religious practices may have become blurred.

We have no way of knowing just how much the Hebrews borrowed from the cult practices of worship of fertility deities. Scripture shows the situation became a matter of concern several times over the years among the Hebrews, as well as during Paul's times in the New Testament.

Next, there is a specific passage of note in Leviticus. It must be remembered the Levitical texts were written to support the Hebrew religion in the face of idolatrous influence. The specific text to which we will refer in this book appears in a section of Leviticus known as the "Holiness Code." This is of particular interest when considering the fact many Biblical scholars believe the Holiness Code was recorded during the Babylonian exile.

It's believed that while the Jews were being held captive in Babylon the Hebrew priests developed the Holiness Code to purify and protect the culture and the religion. The present form of Leviticus could not have been recorded before the exile because there is a clear reference to it in Leviticus 26: 43-44.[7]

TOUGH TIMES IN BABYLON

It was during the Babylonian exile many of the most learned and talented Hebrews were taken into captivity. There was a great deal of pressure on them to accept Babylonian worship. It was the Babylonian King Nebuchadnezzar who ordered the burning in a fiery furnace of three Hebrew children because they would not bow down to worship an image of gold.

The story of Shadrach Meshach and Abednego is recorded in the third chapter of the book of Daniel. They were captive Hebrews who violated the Babylonian King's edict ordering them to worship his pagan God. The story gives some idea of the pressure brought to bear on the Hebrews to embrace the Babylonian religion:

It is commanded O people nations and languages that at that time ye hear the sound of the comet flute harp sackbut psaltery dulcimer and all kinds of music ye fall down and worship the golden image that Nebuchadnezzar the King hath set up: and whoso falleth not down and worshippeth shall the same hour be cast into the midst of a burning fiery furnace. (Daniel 3: 4-6–KJV)

To drop to pray every time anybody played a sackbut was a pretty tall order. There may have been a lot of musicians frequently holding forth on the sackbut. That was serious business. The three persons in the story were heroes to the Hebrews because they chose even under the threat of death, not to embrace the heathen religion. King Nebuchadnezzar had Shadrach, Meshach, and Abednego thrown into a furnace, but the story in Daniel tells of how an angel delivered them:

Then Nebuchadnezzar was furious with Shadrach Meshach and Abednego and his attitude toward them changed. He ordered the furnace heated seven times hotter than usual and commanded some of the strongest soldiers in his army to tie up Shadrach Meshach and Abednego and throw them into the blazing furnace. So these men wearing their robes trousers turbans and other clothes were bound and thrown into the blazing furnace.

The king's command was so urgent and the furnace so hot that the flames of the fire killed the soldiers who took up Shadrach Meshach and Abednego and these three men firmly tied fell into the blazing furnace.

Then King Nebuchadnezzar leaped to his feet in amazement and asked his advisers "Weren't there three men that we tied up and threw into the fire?" They replied, "Certainly Your Majesty." He said "Look! I see four men walking around in the fire unbound and unharmed and the fourth looks like a son of the gods. (Daniel 3: 19-25–ESV)

The Book of Daniel also records the famous story of Daniel who was thrown into a lion's den for not kneeling to worship Baal. Daniel's encounter with the lions came during the transition period toward the conclusion of the Babylonian exile. As we can see, idol worship was a hot issue in Babylonian exile times.

SEX THE BABYLONIAN WAY

It should be no surprise the Hebrews would associate male-to-male prostitution with Babylonian culture. Babylon approved of large-scale intra-sex prostitution.[8] You will find the Levitical reference to same-sex sexual practices in Leviticus 18: 22 is prefaced at the beginning of the chapter by a prohibition against idol worship which makes clear the purpose of what follows:

> *After the doings of the land of Egypt wherein ye dwelt shall ye not do: and after the doings of the land of Canaan whither I bring you shall ye not do: neither shall ye walk in their ordinances. (Leviticus 18: 3–KJV)*

The obvious purpose of this is to separate Hebrews from foreign cults. Throughout the book of Leviticus, there is a setting apart of the Israelites from the idolatrous heathen. The male-male sexual activity the Hebrews would have seen prominently displayed in Babylon would have been in the form of cult prostitution honoring a Babylonian god.

The concern of the Hebrew leadership was it was spilling over into idolatrous religious practices for some of their own citizens as well as spilling the male seed outside of procreation. One can see what an enormous amount of context is ignored when there is simply proof-texting of a stand-alone Levitical Scripture.

Why would the Christian Church ignore this context of and admonition against idolatry and shift the focus to common sexual practices? Why wouldn't emphasis on the matter of God wanting to be an exclusive deity be more important than what body parts were being used by whom in the offending matter of worship of a foreign god?

10

SPEAKING OF WHORES AND DOGS

Another Scripture in the Old Testament frequently used by those who hope to show God's dislike of homosexual persons is Deuteronomy 23:17-18. That Scripture has been grossly mistranslated and has to do with temple prostitution.

The Hebrews' neighbors in the land of Canaan recognized

various types of male same-sex prostitutes including sacred male prostitutes in their places of worship and this practice even carried over into the Hebrew temple. The Hebrew religious practices for a time even involved sacred prostitution with male prostitutes active in the temple.

Scripture documents the activities that took place during the reign over the Kingdom of Judah of King Rehoboam. Rehoboam was the son of King Solomon by an Ammonite princess Naamah. Of the reign of King Rehoboam, I Kings tells us:

> There were even men in the country who were sacred prostitutes. He copied all of the shameful practices of the nations whom Yahweh had dispossessed for the sons of Israel. (I Kings 14: 24–JB)

Rehoboam's grandson Asa made an unsuccessful attempt to permanently remove the sacred prostitutes from the country, "He drove out of the country the men who had been sacred prostitutes and cleared away all of the idols his ancestors had made." (I Kings 15:12–JB)

We must point out that the King James translation uses the term "sodomites" reflecting the bias of the times for the translation and repeating the mishandling of the Sodom saga as we discussed earlier.

Scriptural descriptions of the reforms of Josiah King of Judah indicate that it was at least 200 years after King Asa's unsuccessful attempts that Judah was finally cleared of male sacred prostitutes:

> He pulled down the house of the sacred male prostitutes which was in the Temple of Yahweh and where the women wove clothes for Asherah. (II Kings 23: 7–JB)

Hear what we are saying here. The three passages listed give good Scriptural documentation for *at least 300 years* of the presence of male sacred prostitutes in the Hebrew Kingdom of Judah at least some of the time in the Temple of Yahweh.

"FINDING" DEUTERONOMY

Interestingly, it was during the reign of Josiah that Deuteronomy was "found." In the eighteenth year of his reign, Josiah ordered a reconstruction of the temple. It was during that process the book of the law was "found." Josiah made quite a production out of the finding of the book and relied on it as the basis for using the power of his government to centralize worship and reinstate religious practices that had long been neglected.[1]

Finding Deuteronomy was quite a coincidence to support King Josiah's desires for solidifying control of the kingdom. It's fascinating to note Deuteronomy may have been found again in the 1800s, and once more in 2021. In 1883 an antiquities dealer named Wilhelm Moses Shapira bought fragments of a scroll found by Bedouins and subsequently took them to the British Museum.

It was thought to be an original Deuteronomy scroll. Skeptics challenged Shapira's story, declared him a fraud, and the scroll fragments were sold cheaply to an unknown buyer. No one seems to know where they are today. Shapira died of suicide without corroboration for his find.

Professor Dr. Idan Dershowitz, Chair of the Hebrew Bible and It's Exegesis at the University of Potsdam has put together convincing evidence the fragments were in fact real, and the oldest writings of their kind ever discovered. They may well be the earliest version of Deuteronomy ever found[2]

Professor Dershowitz's assessment of Shapira's own attempt to transcribe and translate portions of the manuscripts seems to present strong proof they may have been legitimate. They contained elements that could only have been known and analyzed after Shapira's time. He could not have had available data or knowledge to forge them during his lifetime.

Dershowitz also evaluated all that is known about the possible contents of the fragments. He suggests they may have been much earlier than the Deuteronomy we know now and that the "Deuteronomic law code" is missing from this version he refers to as "v".

Dershowitz found rather convincing clues the Deuteronomic texts we know may have undergone some redaction.[3]

We don't include this commentary to disparage the Scriptures. It is just to relay the fact the Bible was an evolutionary process. For anyone who thinks Moses sat down one day and wrote Deuteronomy, it just didn't happen that way. Now we have hints that this book Josiah discovered by such serendipity while revamping the temple could even have been sort of augmented along the way.

Maybe it had even been augmented to the point the laws were added. It has surely been misquoted by those who claim it shows God's great dislike for homosexuals. That just demonstrates how mortals have had their way with texts and how some of what Bible scholars casually refer to as, "glossing" undoubtedly occurred with time.

Here is the Deuteronomy text as it appears in the King James Version today:

> There shall be no whore of the daughters of Israel nor a sodomite of the sons of Israel. Thou shalt not bring the hire of an whore or the price of a dog into the house of the Lord thy God for any vow, for even both these are an abomination unto the Lord thy God. (Deuteronomy 23: 17-18–KJV)

First, remember that "abomination" indicates something that is displeasing to God because it has to do with idol worship. Next, note the translators appear to be in error. The word "sodomite" is translated from the Hebrew word *qadesh*. Even referencing the most standardized and accepted Biblical commentaries, one can find this Hebrew word had primarily to do with things sacred to some deity, not with same-sex sexual practices per se. To translate the feminine form as "whores" and the masculine form as "sodomites" appears to continue a persistent misrepresentation of the original intent.

The persons mentioned were considered an abomination (or *toevah)* because they were engaged in acts that were interpreted as being disgusting to God for the simple reason their activities honored a heathen deity. What is probably a more accurate translation of this passage can be found in the Jerusalem Bible:

> There must be no sacred prostitute among the daughters of Israel and no sacred prostitute among the sons of Israel. (JB)

Were these male sacred prostitutes homosexual? Probably not in the sense we understand the term today. Long-time Fordham University Old Testament theologian Dr. Byron Shafer believes the *King James Version* of the Deuteronomy text can also be judged a mistranslation based on the simple logic that a homosexual priest would not be called upon to participate in a fertility ritual. Shafer writes, "although it's not difficult to imagine the role that a heterosexual male priest might play in a fertility ritual it is difficult to imagine the place of a homosexual priest in such a ritual."

"The King James Version translation 'sodomite,'" says Shafer, "has no contemporary scholarly basis and must be judged a mistranslation."[4].

Another scholar, researcher C.A. Tripp, has indicated his research showed there were acts of oral sex (between males) performed as a part of worship even in the Hebrew temple. His writings reveal this practice was a result of the influence of the pagan neighbors' use of sex in worship. He writes:

But for much of the whole First Temple Period (ending with the Babylonian Exile) the Jews shared many of the sexual ways of their neighbors—including various forms of sexual worship. There were such extremes as male and female sacred prostitution, the introduction of young men to the sexual-religious exaltations of orgasm within the Temple and ceremonial mouth-genital contacts between priests and worshipers.[5]

Next, we turn our attention to what could have been meant by the use of the term "dog" in early Hebrew Scripture. Was the Bible referring to all who engaged in same-sex acts as "dogs"? Concerning the use of the term "dog" in the verse from Deuteronomy that is under discussion, Dr. Byron Shafer has this to say:

"dog" as applied to a pagan priest would have pejorative overtones. The dog was not a beloved animal in Israel and "dog" was a term that Israel applied to enemies and the wicked. However, no evidence exists from which to conclude either that "dog" in Semitic languages had sexual implications, or that cultic personnel dressed like dogs functioned sexually. At most the phrase "the wages of a dog" connotes the pay of a wicked servant of a pagan god.[6]

The Deuteronomy passage is a case of Scripture appearing to have been mistranslated in a prejudicial manner. Responsible Biblical scholarship simply does not support any link between the pagan priests referred to in the text and the term "sodomite." The Scripture does not refer to the actual sex acts of the pagan priests but to the fact they were linked with pagan worship and that these activities were being linked with the worship of the Hebrew God Yahweh.

They may have been heterosexual priests, or they may have been priests engaged in same-gender or bisexual prostitution activity for which the money was given to the Temple. The point of the Scripture is that these pagan activities should not involve children of Israel and the Temple treasury should not benefit from cult prostitution. There is no link whatsoever between this text in Deuteronomy and LGBTQ or gender-irrelevant relationships today.

11

DOING WHAT COMES NATURALLY

We must continually remind ourselves that there is a difference between what is natural and what is good. Nothing is more "natural" than being mauled and eaten by a bear. – Sam Harris

Now to examine some of the Scriptures in the New Testament. In one of those Scriptures, the term "natural" appears. One of the things said about LGBTQ persons is that we are not "natural." Relations between two persons of the same sex are referred to as "unnatural acts." The term even shows up in some modern-day law books in describing certain prohibited activities. This says to us that our very nature goes against nature.

This question of just what is considered by some to be "natural law" has played an important role in the formulation of the Church's attitude toward same-sex relationships.

It is tempting to believe that the religious argument of what is natural or unnatural has been directed only at LGBTQ people.

Truth is, it has been used to support prejudice, segregation, and condemnation for a long time.

In his book, *The Bible Told Them So: How Southern Evangelicals Fought to Preserve White Supremacy*, J. Russell Hawkins of Indiana Wesleyan University solidly documents how pastors in the Southern United States used Biblical references claiming the rules of natural law to counter the civil rights movement and John F. Kennedy's move toward civil rights legislation.

The arguments included numerous references to race as the divine design from God as nature is intended to be. The pastors also cited Scripture to claim God set the races in place with each one having a specific natural purpose. They cited Scripture to claim that humans were separated into species by Godly creation just like plants and animals, to exist separately, and in an order of dominance and priority.

"Great mountains and oceans were created," they argued, "to provide a natural barrier and separation for these races and species." The Southern US preachers claimed the natural order designated by the creator could even be judged by which species (or humans) were more successful and dominant. Among other Scriptures used to support this, they cited "By their fruits, ye shall know them."[1]

It was a Biblical justification for White Supremacy based on a very finite view of racial success.

WHAT IS NATURAL ANYWAY?

If we turn to the apostle Paul, he explains to us in I Corinthians 11: 14 that "nature teaches us that long hair dishonors a man." Compare that with Samson's statement in Judges 16: 17 "...a razor has never come on my head for I have been a Nazarite to God from my mother's womb." Was it unnatural for Samson to have long hair? (Remember he lost his great strength when his hair was cut.)

Wouldn't it seem that nature shows us hair grows long? Paul however tells us, according to nature so far as he is concerned, having long hair dishonors a man. It would also seem nature would show us circumcision is unnatural. The writings of Paul however indicate to us that it is natural for Jews and unnatural for Gentiles to be circumcised. Could this be because it simply ran contrary to the Gentiles' nature?

How can we make sense of this business of naturalness? Perhaps, when Paul uses the term "natural," he refers to accepted social practices of the time rather than the divine scheme of things in nature.

The Scripture most used for proof texting concerning nature is this:

And likewise, also the men leaving the natural use of the woman burned in their lust one toward another; men with men working that which is unseemly and receiving in themselves that recompense of their error which was meet. (Romans 1:27–KJV)

We have already explored extensively the belief of the ancient Hebrews that the only natural and acceptable use of the male seed is to be planted into a fertile woman. It's also true the only "natural" sexual use of a woman in that way of thinking would have been as the recipient of that seed. As one can see, any sexual activity that did not fit this definition would not be considered acting according to how God intended. Thus, it would have been contrary to the concept of "nature" at the time and in that setting.

It would be senseless to argue Paul would not have considered sex activities between males not "natural" if it resulted in ejaculation outside of a fertile woman. Any Hebrew scholar of his time would have viewed it so. It was "wasting" the male seed in the context of the time.

Trouble comes when we confuse the reasons for that with the bigotry against LGBTQ persons we see today. Paul would probably have considered any male sexual activity that did not carry with it the potential for procreation as "unnatural."

Affection between men or male coupling was not the issue (except for the attitude that it was degrading for a man to be treated like a woman). The wasting of the seed was considered a sin whether it was done through same-sex intercourse, masturbation, intercourse with a barren woman, or nocturnal emission.

Paul's use of the term "natural" in Romans I is just as connected with the accepted social practices and understanding of his time as his reference to nature teaching us it dishonors a man to have long hair. As translated in our various Biblical versions, the worst he says about the "unnatural" practices is that they are in "error."

NICE WIFE, NICE SISTER

Evangelicals tend to mix Old Testament and New Testament concepts in characterizing "natural." Consider the line you may have heard from some TV evangelists that "God made Adam and Eve, not Adam and Steve." Persons who use that line would have us believe the way things should be by nature is modeled on the Garden of Eden creation story.

The words most quoted by fundamentalists as God's directive about the social place of the sexes were not spoken by God, but by Adam. It is the first declaration of complementarianism patriarchy, not by God, but by a man:

> And *Adam* said, This is now bone of my bones, and flesh of my flesh: she shall be called Woman, because she was taken out of Man. Therefore shall a man leave his father and his mother, and shall cleave unto his wife: and they shall be one flesh. Genesis 2:23-24–KJV

What did Adam mysteriously know about "father" and

"mother" at that point? In the presence of an almighty creator God, what was he doing making such proclamations, just having come from dust, as it were? Maybe, no one was there writing this all down. Are we to believe God or some onlooker later told some Old Testament writer, "Oh, by the way, this is what Adam said"?

In consideration of a Biblical creation story, we are asked to believe God created all the cosmos with one word. Then God stooped into the mud and fashioned one man. Next, for some unexplained reason, there needed to be a rib from the man to make a woman (but only in one of the Genesis creation stories). Then Adam stood and made some sweeping proclamation about the sexes. This duality of the conception of humankind comes from the fact there are two creation stories. In one, humankind is formed from the dust of the earth with no distinction as to woman being made of man. In the other, we find the rib surgery and cloning situation.

There is however one point some commentators seem to over-look: how did the human species go on from there? Cain was the son of Adam and Eve. Who was Cain's wife? Where was the next generation? If we are to believe the Garden of Eden account as it is written, incest must come into the picture somewhere. Cain must have coupled with his sister. I mean, we don't care. Cain didn't have a lot of choices, but does this mean incest as modeled by the creation story is the way nature intended things to be?

Are we to say, "God made Cain and his wife/sister, not Cain and Steve?" Fact is, some ancient Jewish traditions and texts say Adam had a wife before Eve.

Lilith is portrayed there as Adam's first wife. These accounts say she fell from grace to become a demon. Lilith was seen as having wings and as having fallen into being a temptress of mankind. The only place Lilith is mentioned in more modern Bible Scriptures is Isaiah 34:14. She is named then only in some transla-tions. This is another exercise in how translators may have warped things they could not explain to create obscure and widely varied phrases. Here are a few translation versions of the reference to Lilith in Isaiah:

- "Lilith" – **Common English Bible**
- "Lilit (the night monster)" – **Complete Jewish Bible**
- "Lilith" – **Jerusalem Bible**
- "Screech owl" – **King James**
- "Night monster" – **American Standard**
- "Night bird" – **New American Standard**
- (and the best one of all)
- "Night hag" – **Revised Standard**

Did Cain's wife come from Adam's first marriage to Lilith? Some inexplicably attribute Cain's spouse's lineage to "mud people" God made out of the dirt after molding Adam and Eve. It's a stretch, but who knows what else is just mythology? If indeed the creation story is the moral yardstick we're using something goes a little haywire right? What was "natural?"

What was the standard of moral sexuality in the happy garden community? Did Cain marry his demon-spawn half-sister (the daughter of a "night hag")? Is it all mythology? We are simply asked to suspend our disbelief in terms of what God intended to be "natural."

The Lilith story is thought to be an early accounting for the differences in the creation details in Genesis chapter one and Genesis chapter two. In the first chapter, God is said to have made Adam and Eve at the same time. In the second chapter, God made Adam and then fashioned Eve from Adam's rib.

Jewish folklore and ancient Jewish writings reference Lilith as having become a demon. Her description is featured in the *Babylonian Talmud*, but it was not until the *Alphabet of Ben Sira* between the eighth and tenth centuries CE that we see the written story of Lilith as included in the creation accounts brought forward from traditional stories.

There Lilith is said to have abandoned Adam during a disagreement over who should be on top during the sex act. Adam wanted Lilith on the bottom. She would have none of it. In retribution, she became a killer of newborn infants.[2] It may be one of the most extreme "top" versus "bottom" debates in history, and one of the most explicit accounts of retribution from an angry bottom.

The Lilith creation story is feverishly challenged by traditionalists in their effort to distinguish between what was written down when and the understanding of the origins and meaning of ancient folklore contributions to Scripture. A great deal hinges on whether one views the basis of the conflicting Genesis creation stories as being just a product of oral mythology or whether one is looking for inerrant fact.

Of course, another possible explanation for the origins of Cain's wife is that she was the offspring of what Enoch called "The Watchers" or others called "Nephilim" giants.

Mentioned in the Bible and extensively in the Book of Enoch (a canonized ancient Hebrew account) Nephilim were beings from Heaven. Scripture says such beings saw human women as attractive and mated with them:

> the sons of God saw that the daughters of humans were beautiful and they married any of them they chose. Then the Lord said, "My Spirit will not contend with humans forever for they are mortal; their days will be a hundred and twenty years."
>
> The Nephilim were on the earth in those days—and also afterward—when the sons of God went to the daughters of humans and had children by them. They were the heroes of old men of renown. (Genesis 6:2-4–NIV)

The fact is, certain Scriptures were chosen to explain creation for many of us in church school. Whether obvious in Scripture or in ancient inspired sacred writings contemporary with Scripture, there are several things about Hebrew creation mythology that were not pointed out in our religious upbringing.

Those who cling to the Eden creation story as the inerrant model for natural law might tell you God made an exception with Cain's marriage in allowing incest as a way of populating the earth. Please show us the way to the Exception Department. We've been looking for it all day. If God can make an exception to populate the earth why not exceptions to keep the earth from being over-populated?

WHY DOES NATURAL EVEN MATTER?

Some would argue that LGBTQ relationships are unnatural because they do not occur in nature. There are two things wrong with that argument. First, there is a lot of documentation that same-sex sexual activities and love do occur among animals. Second, who said what animals do is the model for what is natural? Would people have us eating our own babies if they are born with some abnormality? That's what some animals do. Is that what being "natural" means?

Should we consider it natural for a female in "heat" to be followed by a pack of males who fight over her? Is that the model for healthy natural heterosexual love? This argument presupposes animals are somehow more natural than humankind. They're not. Where is it written our traits and actions occurring as a part of the human experience are any less natural than the experience of animals?

Since sex acts between persons of the same sex naturally occur and have naturally occurred throughout recorded history, why would they be anything other than natural?

It's particularly interesting to note that some conservative Christians who insist "homosexuality is unnatural" and therefore sinful, will at the same time argue that the nature of humankind is one of sin and moral bankruptcy.

What credibility can there be in an argument that pressures LGBTQ persons to bring their lives into line with what is "natural" for humankind; at the same time claiming what is natural for humankind is sin and rebellion against God? To say the least this definition of "natural" as wholly desirable with the simultaneous suggestion of it being horribly tainted by sin is lacking in reason.

In a continuation of an attack on same-sex marriage, a spokesman for a conservative Catholic organization recently referred to it as "legal fiction." He claimed that the marriage was not according to "natural law" or "God's law," therefor, despite the fact that it was sanctioned by national law in the U.S., it was not legal.

This is a sign of what is coming. Already there are those who have decided they do not need to even honor a law if it is contrary to "natural" law or Biblical law. The term "legal fiction" is a dog whistle that suggests pushing for favorite laws, but picking and choosing which ones to honor.

Would the same people refer to a heterosexual marriage that was not accepted and confirmed in the church as "legal fiction?" It's a slippery slope when folks start deciding their perception of "natural" is the rule of law. It makes the preacher and the judge one and the same. Where else will an idea of "legal fiction" be applied as an excuse for religious disrespect for the law?

Our understanding of naturalness is influenced by our culture. Some of the cultures closest to nature in their way of living may engage in ceremonies involving gashing, cutting, and otherwise inflicting pain. These ceremonies would be considered quite unnatural by what we accept in a civilized society. At the same time, our civilized society views it as perfectly natural that we build and store enough nuclear weapons to destroy our world several times over.

Human and even religious understanding of nature changes. The arguments against Galileo were Bible-based including this: "The sun riseth and goeth down and returneth to his place: and there rising again." (Ecclesiastes 1:5–KJV)

Galileo would argue religion can be wrong when it comes to science and nature. The sun does not revolve around the earth. This is despite the fact some early church Fathers believed that was the natural state of things according to Scripture. Galileo was not absolved of heresy until 1992.

In the dedication of this book is a mention of *Giordano Bruno*. He was executed by the Church in part because he dared to put forward a belief that stars were suns around which planets orbited and that some of those planets might harbor life. He also said the universe was endless and had no center. Charges of other "heresies" were conveniently added to seal his fate. He ultimately recanted everything but the cosmological views.

It would be nice to be able to quote his last words, but the authorities had attached a clamp to his tongue to silence him. He was hung upside down and naked.

Killing him because of a belief he was misrepresenting nature was not an act of a religion reflecting the nature of God. It was an act of ignorance, protection of power, and cruelty in the name of Jesus. It was a sinful act by the church leaders. It was a proud expression of stupidity based on uninformed ancient proclamations about nature. It was also an act that may have set humanity's understanding of the cosmos back for hundreds of years.

Researcher Daniel Helminiak gives this perspective on science and the sexual revolution:

> We had misconceived the natural order. We misunderstood the nature that the laws of nature express. Thus, like displacing the Earth from the center of the universe, the Sexual Revolution seems to turn the old order upside down.
>
> Accordingly at the apex, the most important, the defining purpose of human sex, would be a spiritual matter: interpersonal union, the communion of lovers, the sex-induced weaving of dreams and sharing of promises, the envisioning of new possibilities.[3]

12

PAUL'S CHURCH NEWSLETTERS

Now let's turn to other New Testament proof texting and specifically to some discussion of the Apostle Paul. Remember, it is important to understand the Bible in the context of the times, the people, the circumstances under which it was written, and the surrounding Scripture. We are aspiring in this book to cover the context of Biblical interpretation like a journalist would cover a story to provide good reader understanding. A story sometimes needs a backgrounder. (Convincing evidence suggests much of what is attributed to Paul was not written by him but we will proceed with our discourse here as if it were.)

Paul was a Roman citizen and a Jew. He was born Saul of Tarsus and Tarsus was in what is now Turkey. As a Jew, Paul was strongly schooled in all the meticulous Jewish Laws. He was mentored by Gamaliel the First, a renowned Rabbi and member of the local Sanhedrin or Jewish high court of the territory.

KNOCKED OFF HIS HORSE

Tradition tells us Saul was touring the country with the purpose of persecuting Christians when, as the story goes, he was blinded and knocked off his horse by a great light. He was converted in the process to Christianity.

He later regained his sight, changed his name from Saul to Paul, and positioned himself as a leader of the Christian church. All of this is recounted in the book of Acts.

Now we are going to report on this matter of Paul's letters that make up much of the New Testament. We'll dissect them, consider them in context, and go over the meaning of the language. All of this is done in what has become an obligatory exercise for LGBTQ Christians. We, however, will approach all of this as a journalist looking for the facts behind the story. Before doing that, let's just set the stage.

LETTERS ALL ABOUT CONGREGATIONAL BROUHAHA

By whatever means (partly because he had the distinction of being both a Jew and a Roman citizen) Paul had become a leader of this far-flung-loose-knit doctrinal association that was the early Christian Church. The Christian churches were pretty much a mess at that point. The fellowship had recruited Jews, Romans, and Greeks. They all came from different social and religious backgrounds and religious traditions.

While some of the Jewish converts were sanctimoniously clinging to the strict traditions of the Jewish law, others had been swooned by the Gentile cultures and assimilated into various Roman and Greek practices. The churches had become a hodgepodge of sundry traditions and were fighting among themselves.

In some, there was embraced the common tradition of the locals to have sex in various temples as a way of worship. In many, there was constant infighting between the cultural and religious factions as to what was sin and what wasn't. There was debate as to how much of the Jewish law the Greeks had to endure, even to the point of circumcision for adult males.

Now Paul, ever the intellectual and the peacemaker, was trying to sort all of this out by sending in what we might call the first church newsletters. It was a herculean task. He had to continue to enjoy congregations' high esteem but, at the same time, break the various factions loose from their dogmatic clinging to the divisive righteous indignation aimed at protecting what they believed to be appropriate religious behavior and tradition.

Imagine a church where one faction is saying, "We can't have a fulfilling worship service without honoring God with a little public sex." And another faction is thinking, "that dirty little uncircumcised sinner brought a bacon sandwich to our church social."

As we said, Paul was trying to be a diplomat to sort all of this out in a spirit of Christian love and for the survival of the church. In this setting, it's fascinating to look at the writings attributed to him and notice Paul (or whoever wrote the letters) specifies certain statements are "from the Lord" and others are simply his own opinion.

For example, in I Corinthians 7:10 (JB) Paul instructs those who are married saying, "This is not from me but from the Lord."

About celibacy, he says in verse 25, "I have no directions from the Lord but give my own opinion" (*JB*).

We know we do not have actual manuscripts from Paul. We do see suggestive evidence that apparently when he was speaking on an important matter and wanted to emphasize his direction "from the Lord" he specified that (at least in the versions we have). Paul (as represented in the Scriptures we have) makes no claim to having had a "direction from the Lord" about same-sex relationships.

Three New Testament proof texts (all of them purported to be written by Paul) are used to justify the condemnation of same-sex sexual acts. They appear in Paul's letters to the early churches.

It's important to remember Paul did not sit down one day and say, "I think I'll write some things that would be nice to have in the Bible forever." He was a minister and a respected leader in the early church. He purportedly wrote letters to the early Christian churches to share news, give advice and instruction, greet his sisters and brothers, and encourage the churches in the faith.

There has also been a great deal of theological scholarly debate as to what letters were or were not actually written by Paul. Thirteen letters in the New Testament claim to have been written by the Apostle himself. Even the most conservative scholars generally agree that only seven of them hold up to evidentiary examination they may have been *copied* from something written by Paul.

These are Romans, First and Second Corinthians, Galatians, Philippians, I Thessalonians, and Philemon. Six others were probably not. These are known in Biblical scholarship as the "deutero-Pauline" letters.

Although there is debate about when they were written, who wrote them, and under what circumstances, there seems to be strong scholarly evidence the writer(s) of all of them was(were) not Paul.[1] There is more than a little suspicion some of the Pauline letters were forged, augmented, or revised according to the purpose of later church leaders.

We, however, are just going to proceed here as if they were

indeed written by this Christian Roman Jew from what is now Turkey going (for some reason) under the assumed name of Paul. We will continue as if it doesn't make any difference whether there is controversy concerning their origin. We are also going to assume for this writing the letters meant exactly what they said to exactly whom they were written.

In the words of New Testament theologian Adolph Deissman:

> The letters of Paul are not literary; they are real letters, not epistles; they were written by Paul not for the public and posterity but for the persons to whom they are addressed. Almost all of the mistakes that have ever been made in the study of St. Paul's life and work have arisen from the neglect of the fact that his writings are non-literary and letter-like in character.[2]

SPECIFIC LETTERS TO SPECIFIC PEOPLE ABOUT SPECIFIC CIRCUMSTANCES

In looking at the writings of Paul we must see them considering this fact: They respond to specific requests for information and discuss specific problems in specific churches.

Suppose Paul sat down to write to the Galatian Christians and the Thessalonian Christians at the same time (which of course was probably not the case). And suppose further that when he addressed the packets in which the letters had been placed for delivery he mistakenly wrote: "To the Thessalonians" on the letter intended for Galatia, and To the Galatians" on the letter intended for the Thessalonians.

What would have happened when the Thessalonians (between whom and Paul there were strong and mutual bonds of love and affection) opened the letter addressed to them and found the sarcastic words Paul had intended for the Galatians?[3]

Existing simultaneously in similar cultures those two churches had much more in common than we would have with either one of them today. Despite their commonality, the Thessalonian church and the Galatian church had different problems. There were enough differences between them that it would have been difficult for one church to identify with comments Paul had written to the other. Someone receiving a misaddressed letter would not be familiar with the circumstances being addressed.

Paul was not represented as having set out to write generic form letters addressed "to whom it may concern." It was not his intention to write messages eternally valid for all situations and all churches everywhere for all ages.

Paul's letters do carry messages for us today. These are messages addressed to specific circumstances in churches of his time. If we find important and eternal truths in them, so much the better. These, however, must be viewed in the light of the time in which the letters were written and the circumstances they addressed.

Take a modern example. Suppose a district church fellowship official had written responding to a letter from a small rural church in the 1800s. The church wanted to know how to deal with the problem of horses wandering around outside the building during services. The district official wrote back stating "horses should be tied in front of the church."

How much sense would it make for someone reading that in the twenty-first century to believe all churches should have horses tied in front of them all the time? The same kind of logic is used when some people try to apply the letters of Paul to modern circumstances with no regard for their original intent and meaning.

Paul was addressing things within the scope of his experience. He never claimed to be addressing anything else or to be writing to anyone else but the addressees in the letters. It seems reasonable to believe he would probably have been shocked to think people centuries later would be clinging to weird translations of every word people claim he wrote as being the "words of God."

He might have been even more horrified to think insisting on strict adherence to his teachings (or forgeries of letters said to be from him) would take place with inadequate thought to the context or circumstance under which the letters were written. The next few chapters walk through the context surrounding Paul's letters and give you some idea of his influences and thinking in his time.

13

ABUSING YOURSELF WITH ALL MANKIND!

In First Corinthians 6:9-10 is one of the New Testament proof texts used most frequently to denounce same-sexuality as unchristian. Before examining the text, we'll report on the circumstances under which it was written. The text appears in one of Paul's letters to the church at Corinth.

HEY SAILOR!

Corinth was a seaport a cultural crossroads of its time. The city was on the Isthmus of Corinth, the shortest route from Europe to Asia. This geographic position caused numerous cultures to be represented in Corinth's population.

There were all sorts of religions. To the south of the city, there rose the mountains of the Peloponnesus, the most prominent of which was Acrocorinth. This peak was the site of many pagan temples.

We know from literature and archaeology the city was dotted with temples to various gods. In I Corinthians 8:5 Paul refers to these "gods and lords in plenty." Archaeologists have unearthed remains of the seven columns of the temple of Apollo. There were also temples to Athena, Poseidon, Asklepios, and others.

High atop the Acrocorinth was the temple of Aphrodite the goddess of love. Here, no fewer than a thousand slave girls served as hierodules (sacred slaves) attached to the service of the temple and of the worshippers who utilized their services in orgiastic worship activities.

Corinth was widely known as a city of pleasure and vice. A Greek proverb said that not everyone should go to Corinth. The city even found its way into the Greek language with *korinthia kore* (Corinthian girl) which meant prostitute *korinthiastes* (Corinthian businessman) which meant whoremonger and *korinthtazesthat* (to play the Corinthian) which meant to visit a house of prostitution.

There was scarcely a more unlikely place in the Greco/Roman world for the Gospel to find favorable reception.[1] Corinth was well-known for its brothels (both male and female) that lined the walk to the Acrocorinth. "Corinthian" became a Greek slang term for the sexually loose.

Just as the temple of Aphrodite was dedicated to female beauty, so was the temple of Apollo dedicated to male beauty. Here also sex was glorified and nude statues of Apollo in various poses of virility "fired his male worshippers to physical displays of devotion with the god's beautiful boys."[2]

Although in Paul's time years of Roman rule had been thought to have cleaned up the city a bit, Corinth was still a seaport town with lots of sailors, lots of forms of prostitution, and continuing association of prostitution with religious worship. The same-sex activity Paul would have encountered during his missionary visits there would have been associated with idolatry, pederasty, or prostitution, and sometimes all of the above.

Many of the liaisons common in Corinth were also adulterous in nature. Many, if not most, of the men who had young male lovers or who engaged in same-sex activities in the temples would have had wives and children at home. These sexual practices also frequently involved slavery. Many young boys were purchased through the slave trade and castrated to preserve their youthful appearance for the pleasure of their masters.[3]

One highly respected New Testament scholar Robin Scroggs has extensively studied male same-sex relations in New Testament times. He strongly expresses a belief there was only one basic model for male same-sex sexual activity in the Greco-Roman world and that was pederasty. He says when the New Testament makes mention of male intra-sex acts it must be speaking of pederasty because that was the only model in the times.

Scroggs points out the enormous differences between the actions attacked by the New Testament and the practices of today's LGBTQ community. Because of this, he says, "Biblical judgments against homosexuality are not relevant to today's debate."[4]

The society in Corinth was one in which sexual activity was routinely a part of worship. It may be difficult to imagine that any Christian church might have encountered problems such as persons wanting to have sex as a part of the service. In Corinth, such a thing might have occurred in the Christian church as a matter of routine.

In a city whose very name was synonymous with prostitution, it's reasonable to think Paul would address the issue of male cult prostitution. After all, Paul wrote these letters to a church surviving in an atmosphere that would make Mardi Gras in New Orleans look like a Mennonite church picnic.

One of the specific problems addressed by Paul was the fact that a kind of libertine attitude had arisen in the church in Corinth. Paul in his letter to the Galatians felt a need to tell them not to give up their liberty but in Corinth, it was an entirely different story. Paul was moved to tell the Corinthians they had taken this liberty business a bit too far. We must realize what they might have seen as liberties in their time and what we might see today as a rather liberated approach to worship, are two enormously different things.

In that city, there were people newly converted to Christianity who had been accustomed to having sex as a part of religious worship. It should not tax our imagination to think some may have believed this is what should be done in the Christian church.

"Brethren we have met to worship" had a totally different meaning in this context. They may have thought this sex in church was liberty as well as nicely competitive for raising a little money in the offering plate. These people were accustomed to mixing religions and having many gods and many different forms of worship.

Some were tempted to be Christian while still going over to the pagan temple to worship Apollo by engaging the prostitutes there. Now a text from I Corinthians:

> "Know ye not that the unrighteous shall not inherit the Kingdom of God? Be not deceived: neither fornicators nor idolators nor adulterers nor effeminate nor abusers of themselves with mankind nor thieves nor covetous nor drunkards nor revilers nor extortioners shall inherit the Kingdom of God" (I Corinthians 6: 9- 10–KJV).

To examine the variations and (perhaps) find out if there may have been prejudice displayed by various Bible translators, it's important here to dissect terms a little bit.

AUTHORITIES CAN'T AGREE

The various versions of the words we see in the King James Version as "effeminate" and "abusers of themselves with mankind" are translated intentionally and differently in subsequent English language versions of the Bible. The New International Version for example translates both words as "homosexual offender." What in the world," one might ask, "is a 'homosexual offender?'" Is that someone who offends homosexuals?

In his book *What the Bible Really Says About Homosexuality*, Vatican-educated theologian Daniel Helminiak points out:

> The Catholic Church's recent New American Bible invites the same cynicism. It translated arsenokoitai as "practicing homosexuals." How amazing! A first-century text would now seem to teach what Roman Catholicism began teaching only in the mid-1970s: to be homosexual is no fault but to engage in homosexual acts is wrong."[5]

In his words, it's an attempt to "nuance the translation." Nuance the translation to say the least. There is a certain fluidity that appears to be heavily practiced when translators come upon anything that might be linked to LGBTQ. There seems to be quite a lot of translation nuancing.

Simply put, Paul is just listing all the ways he could think of one might "waste" the male seed and he's condemning pagan temple prostitution for practicing idolatry.

ALL GREEK TO TOO MANY

Just as everyone seems forced to do on this subject, we are going to jump into a discussion of the original Greek Bible words. The Greek translation discussion is all here; help yourself if you want to. It is ridiculous to even have to write it and here's why: The mainstream big production Bible translators appear to this writer to maybe be acting like little Sneaky Petes on this issue. One could argue it all day long, but no one knows for sure what Paul's original letters said in ancient Greek words (if they even were Paul's letters and whichever version one might be "translating).

Many theology and linguistic scholars now agree with the more LGBTQ-favorable understanding of this text, but it's translated to modern English in a way that could prompt even scholars in ancient Greek to hold weekend seminars with hours of discussion.

What one could seem to hope for is an honest and unbiased effort at translation. Don't get your hopes too high. It doesn't always happen.

FORNICATORS AND OTHER HETEROSEXUAL PERVERTS

As an example, let's look at the King James Version of the Corinthians Scripture. There is the word "fornicators." It is clear that in English a "fornicator" is someone who has sex or has had sex outside of marriage. That includes pre-marital sex. That's just the English language. It's what it means. This person might have a proclivity to have sex without being married. If they lust after having sex outside of marriage maybe that makes them a "fornicator."

Notice the verse goes on to say "adulterers." Several Scriptures in the Bible reference "fornication" and then "adultery" as two terms in the same sentence. That would seem to mean "fornicator" is having non-marital sex somehow separate from adultery. It comes from a Greek word from which we get "porn." If one were to look at all porn sites and see everything done there, that is apparently what this Greek word conveyed. It was pretty lusty.

Just like all of Paul's words in this Scripture, it was used to raise folks' eyebrows and fire up their indignation to set them up for Paul's subsequent indictment of hypocrisy that followed.

The point is, the sin pointed out by Paul as translated in the King James Version here is not just the act of fornication it is being a "fornicator." That is, we suppose, having a fornicator orientation. Or it could even be a self-avowed fornicator. If a "fornicator" does not engage in fornication lately, he/she is still a "fornicator" right?

Maybe they have a "fornicator lifestyle." If one is a "fornicator" but does not engage in acts of fornication, is it still a sin? Maybe it ultimately drives one to mortal sin. Nobody seems to be writing book after book on that one. A fornicator is a fornicator. Right? Not necessarily.

While the translators seem to have narrowed the translations in another part of the verse and even combined Greek words to justify singling out "homosexuals," they appear to have really (intentionally perhaps) left this "fornicator" business quite ambiguous. In these translations "fornicator" becomes:

Translations:

- "...sexually immoral" – NIV
- "...indulge in sexual sin" – NLT
- "...sexually immoral" – ESV
- "...fornicators" –NAS
- "...people who are immoral" – GNT
- "...whoremongers" – LITV
- "...fornicators" –ASV
- "...people of immoral lives " – JB

Those cover quite a lot of territory. Nowhere does anyone say, "people who have non-marital sex" or "anyone who has unusual sex outside of marriage." Notice two of those translations just generally refer to people who are "immoral." That is such a broad generalization. Nowhere does any translation say, "heterosexuals who nastily play around outside of marriage."

Maybe the translation could be "heterosexual offenders." Maybe a heterosexual fornicator who is a woman is an "abuser of herself with men." (Just gotta love the *Literal Standard Version* of "whoremongers"! That's a pimp, right?)

Just considering Paul's ancient Hebrew-based belief that spilling the male seed outside a fertile woman was a transgression should bring a fuller understanding of the use of the word that the *King James Version* and others translated as "fornicator." It would make a lot of common sense. Why would the translators not give us more to work with here?

"Immoral" is a translation, but obviously, it is not cut-and-dried. Even if the proper translation is "engage in immorality," one would still have to believe it is any sex outside of marriage. How is that differentiated from adultery? We simply need to look at what was considered "morality" sexually. It was strictly sex within marriage (not during menses). Anything other than that would be immorality. Sex outside of marriage is fornication but somehow that is separated in this Scripture from "adultery."

Does that mean immorality is just generally being nasty? Most of the translations don't heap guilt on anyone specifically for this. Of course, proof texting Christians who have sex before or outside marriage don't want to be considered "fornicators." It was just "immorality" or an isolated individual incidence of fornication.

Fornicator is an identity. Immorality is an act or condition. That is the subtle difference in what could appear to be a translator's bias.

In Paul's frame of thought, people who indulged in sexual sin would have been anyone who wasted the male seed. Maybe some of our modern Bible translators have at some point in their lives engaged in non-marital sex, thus making them a fornicator. Perhaps they longed at some time to spill their male seed outside of a fertile woman. Fornicator! Maybe they did "waste" their seed in such a way. That would be indulging in sexual sin in Paul's terms. They will not inherit the kingdom of God. Sad!

As was said in an earlier chapter, the real question to ask is, "Why are LGBTQ people treated differently?" Instead of a generalization that defies specificity and is used regarding what could be heterosexual extra-marital sex, the translators narrow in and become very confident in their translating where "homosexuality" is concerned. Notice some are acts, one is a profession, and some are identities. Even then there appears to be subjectivity more than agreement:

Translations:

- "...men who have sex with men" – NIV
- "...are male prostitutes or practice homosexuality" – NLT
- "...men who practice homosexuality" – ESV
- "...abusers of themselves with men" – ASV
- "...homosexual perverts" – GNT
- "...effeminate nor sodomites" – LITV
- "...homosexuals" – NAS
- "...catamites sodomites" – JB
- "... sexual perverts" – RSV

Notice the variety. Note some get around the "homosexual" orientation vs. "homosexual acts" very precisely: "men who practice homosexuality." It just seems quite contrived. On the other hand, the translators could split hairs in the other part of the verse and say, "those who practice fornication." That would get the former fornicators off the hook (if they don't practice fornication today). One could then say, "they're not fornicators, their just OSFA (Opposite Sex Fornicator Attracted). Instead, it just becomes "immorality."

Notice particularly the *Revised Standard Version (RSV)* translation as "sexual perverts." *A Revised Standard Version* initial inclusion of the term "homosexual" in New Testament translations is the subject of a documentary entitled "*1946*" released in 2021. The documentary is produced by Sharon "Rocky" Roggio and is based on research by Kathy Baldock and Ed Oxford. In preparation for their book *Forging a Sacred Weapon: How the Bible became anti-gay*, Baldock and Oxford uncovered controversy surrounding the 1946 introduction of the term "homosexual" as a translation of words in I Corinthians 6:9-10 in the RSV Bible version.

The documentary even includes a revelation that a member of that translation team sent an impassioned letter to his fellow team members pleading with them not to include the word "homosexual" in the translation. The video also reveals that the RSV team did ultimately agree to change the term to "sexual perverts" but not until after the "homosexual" word as a translation had been in the RSV for twenty-five years. Unfortunately, it had already been picked up by numerous other translations and it was too late to reverse that course.[6]

Researchers Kathy Baldock and Ed Oxford who contributed research for the documentary movie *1946* have said that German translators made an even greater error. The earlier German version of Leviticus says, "Man shall not lie with *young boys* as he does with a woman, for it is an abomination." The several New Testament Scriptures that translate into German the Greek *arsenokoitai* also attribute it to boy molesting. That's because it was translated to the German word "knabenschander." "Knaben" is boy, "schander" is molester. This dates at least as far back as the days of Martin Luther. It seems the German translation in both the Old and New Testaments didn't even move to the German language equivalent of "homosexual" until 1983.[7] Previously, someone in German had just decided the original Greek was talking about "knabenschander."

LESBIANS AS COLLATERAL DAMAGE

To combine Paul's Greek words and simply come up with "homosexual" or "practice homosexuality" as some translators do incorporates lesbian women. How is a lesbian somehow inappropriately effeminate or abusing herself with mankind? Even if one understands the translation to mean soft, or practicing anal intercourse, or being a male temple prostitute, how can anyone jump to the idea Paul was talking about lesbian women? Lesbians are just sucked into the vortex of the (suspect) Bible translation.

Of course, some translators leave lesbians out by specifying "homosexual men." Others just heap the lesbians into Paul's sinful pile and disregard any potential for outfall from that. It's "homosexuals," or "homosexual perverts."

Probably no fifteen-year-old lesbian girl being pelted with Scripture is going to say, "According to the original Greek, Paul wasn't talking about me." Chances are anyone quoting the Scripture to her will just go right to the translation that lumps all "homosexuals" in together in one term.

Remember, there is a 960-page catalog that lists English translation versions of the Bible and over 5000 discordant Greek manuscripts from which they are drawn. If anyone ever had any questions about how the transcription and translation of the Bible might have been nuanced over the centuries by humankind (men), one might cite this strange incorporation of lesbians in Paul's letter (as "homosexuals") as a good example.

Finally, was Paul talking about anal intercourse? You don't see that translation. Anal intercourse can be, and is, practiced by heterosexuals. To this casual observer, it appears great effort is made to specifically target this Corinthians Scriptural admonition at LGBTQ people.

Some translations specify men, some specify the act and not the proclivity, some specify male prostitution, and some just happily incorporate women as "homosexuals" with no justification whatsoever, all based on the same Greek text.

THE ABSURDLY OBLIGATORY EXERCISE IN GREEK WORDS

Notice in some modern translations two Greek words become one, as in the NAS version where the word "homosexuals" is used. The various Bible translations are taken from two Greek words. They are *malakoi* and *arsenokoitai* The word *malakoi* is translated in the *King James Version* to mean "effeminate." It is a Greek word literally meaning "soft."

We find the same word translated differently in other places in the New Testament:

Jesus began to say unto the multitudes concerning John what went ye out in the wilderness to see? A reed shaken with the wind? But what went ye out to see? A man clothed in soft (malakoi) raiment.? Behold they that wear soft (malakoi) clothing are in kings' houses." (Matthew 11: 7-8–KJV)

He began to speak unto the people concerning John what went ye out in the wilderness to see? A reed shaken with the wind? But what went ye out to see? A man clothed in soft raiment (malakoi)? Behold they who are gorgeously appareled and live delicately are in kings' courts. (Luke 7: 24-25–KJV)

Now, in some wild stretch of the imagination some translator could just decide to be consistent in translation and suggest Jesus was asking whether people were going out in the wilderness to see a dressed up "homosexual," a "homosexual pervert," somebody masturbating, or just someone having some anal sex with a German boy. That would put a little different tone on that verse, wouldn't it? That is where the inconsistency in translation becomes emphasized.

It's easy to see from these passages the word *malakoi* has to do with fancy clothing. It appears to be associated with royalty. Men who engaged in same-sex activities were not always thought of as effeminate or royal. Historian John Boswell tells us, "many hetero-sexual men were called effeminate by ancient writers and there is no essential connection between inappropriate gender behavior and sexual preference in any ancient literature."

Boswell says *malakoi* was used to put down people for numerous reasons in ancient literature and it is difficult to prove any link between the word and gay people. "In the absence of such proof," he writes, "the soundest inference is that *malakoi* refers to general moral weakness with no specific connection to homosexuality."[8] Maybe, just maybe, it could be translated as "immoral."

The word effeminate usually meant "self-indulgent" or "voluptuous" even as late as the seventeenth century.[9] It is likely the *King James* translators meant to convey that meaning rather than referring to same-sex relations in I Corinthians 6:9. Perhaps since self-indulgence is far more widespread than homosexuality tagging this Scripture onto a scapegoat segment of the population helped a large number of people to escape condemnation.[10]

It's important to note that *malakoi* is interpreted by some writers within the Orthodox Christian church to mean masturbation. *The Rudder (Padaliort) the Book of Canons of the Holy Catholic and Apostolic Church of the Orthodox Christians* footnotes a canon concerning masturbation and the Corinthians Scripture we cited as follows:

> Though St. Chrysostom interpreted the Greek word here for "masturbators" (which also signifies "soft") to mean "men who have become prostitutes," while Theophylactus explains it as meaning "those who suffer obscene treatment" (i.e. catamites) yet many teachers have taken the word to be used in the sense herein attached to it i.e. that of masturbator.[11]

A note in *The Rudder* from the translator goes on to say the word *malakoi* has mistakenly been thought by Bible translators to mean "soften" but has been in common use in Greek as a euphemism for masturbation. [12] The canon of the Greek Orthodox Church as written in that publication also directs men masturbating each other should have an imposition of up to eight days of penance.[13]

Although some scholars would discount the use of this reference as being from an era of Greek language other than Bible times, we can ask whether the Greeks would speak with some authority on the meaning of Greek usage of Greek words. Theirs is a language that has remained closer to its early roots than most others, and modern Greek speakers can read and understand a significant percentage of words in the early language. We acknowledge that syntax changes over time, but we also provide here an example of how a modern church with deep ancient roots may interpret these concepts.

It makes sense. The prohibition of masturbation would be a repeat of Old Testament prohibitions against the "spilling of seed." It would also be based on the same incorrect biological assumptions discussed earlier; that spilling the male seed is somehow murder and the male seed alone contains all the elements of procreation and need only be planted into a female body to grow into a child.

It apparently doesn't matter which sex you are thinking about when you are masturbating. It's depicted in *The Rudder,* for example, as a devastating habit. It's clear the mistaken biological assumptions upon which the rules against the spilling of seed in both the Old and New Testaments were based make them invalid as prohibitions in the light of modern understanding. Their applicability to our lives must be viewed in consideration of their historical, medical, and scientific context.

It's also clear there is feigned confusion among Biblical scholars as to the exact meaning of the word *malakoi.* To translate the word as "effeminate" or as simply "homosexual" misses most of the meaning historically ascribed to the word.

NASTY MALE #^(%{^&S

The second term *arsenokoitai* is translated by the *King James Version* as "abusers of themselves with mankind." *Arsenokoitai* refers to the sexual role of the male. It may have been coined by Paul or picked up by Paul in Corinth where it may have been common street slang. No one has a way of knowing exactly what it meant. Indications are it was a lusty word.

It is particularly interesting that the book of Orthodox canons

(*The Rudder*) specifically uses the more modern term *"arsenocoetia"* as an act for which certain penance was specified. The canons seem to divide the act of *"arsenocoetia"* into two types. One is man-on-man, and the other is man-on-woman. Curiously the penance is greater for the active partner than the passive partner in male-male encounters.

The judgments of the church are harsher for a man who practices *arsenocoetia* with a strange woman than with another man. The penalties are harsher still for a man who engages in *arsenocoetia* with his wife.[14] It seems obvious in those canons that *arsenocoetia* refers to anal intercourse. This would seem to make it clear any translation of this as simply "homosexuals" is way off base.

The harsher penalties for performing this act with women seem a strong indication the prohibition has more to do with the spilling of the male seed and wasting a woman's participation as an interruption of the reproductive process than it does with intimate contact between persons of the same sex.

We hasten here again to point out that the Orthodox text cited using *arsenocoetia* is not ancient Greek as utilized in the writings of the New Testament. It is also true it has centuries of church tradition as a background and represents some level of Greek understanding of a term.

(Note: This same discussion can apply to I Timothy 1:10 where the word *arsenokoitai* translated as "them that defile themselves with mankind." is used.) If one were to consider what the Greek canons seem to suggest, maybe the Scripture should read "masturbators nor those who practice anal sex." This still wouldn't get folks out of the sin bin, but it would lump together as equal, two things treated quite differently by the modern churches. It would also throw heterosexuals into the mix. (The gentle religious reader is invited to suspend disbelief here and realize a significant number of heterosexuals do engage in anal sex.)

It does not appear to be the best scholarship to simply combine the two words *malakoi* and *arsenokoitai* and translate them as "homosexuals." It seems lazy scholarship at best and politically motivated crusading at worst. One could even believe it to be a biased translation, considering our earlier discussion of how translators seem to get fornicators off the hook.

There is no doubt that in Corinth there were sexual activities practiced that were idolatrous, demeaning, cruel, and disgusting. One cannot transpose what Paul was saying to the church at Corinth into an indictment of a loving compassionate LGBTQ relationship as people know in our society.

The Corinthian Scripture points up the importance of understanding the Bible in historical context. A closer reading of Paul reveals he is not so heavily interested in condemnation. In I Corinthians 6: 12 (just three verses away from the text we just discussed) Paul says everything is in play legally for him: "All things are lawful for me but not all things are profitable. All things are lawful for me, but I will not be mastered by anything." (NAS)

14

NAUGHTY IN ROME

In examining the next proof text Scriptures we should realize the letter to the Romans was written in Corinth.[1] It was in this atmosphere of paganism and sexual laxity in Corinth that Paul dictated his letter to the church in Rome. This was probably rather appropriate. Let's pay a little visit to ancient Rome.

It is, of course, important to consider the Roman environment as we look at the text. The Roman culture was rife with pagan worship and prostitution.

EMPERORS WITH ISSUES

Rome was entertained by the antics of its emperors. They were viewed as gods. Their statues were erected in temples and worshipped. The issue of idolatry was particularly sensitive to Jews because of the threat these statues would be erected in Jewish places of worship.

It would not be surprising for Paul to link same-sex activities to emperor worship. Throughout history, bisexuality was common-place among Roman emperors. Claudius is said to have been the only emperor who was "100 percent heterosexual"[2] and he was a sadist who had people tortured in his presence and enjoyed watching bloody and sadistic executions.[3]

Caligula occasionally made Caesonia, the woman to whom he was married, dress in military uniforms. He is said to have had male lovers and to have sometimes dressed in drag.[4] He often danced at night and once at the close of the second watch summoned three senators of consular rank to the palace.

> Arriving half dead with fear, they were conducted to a stage upon which amid a tremendous racket of flutes and heel taps Caligula suddenly burst in dressed in cloak and ankle-length tunic, performed a song and dance and disappeared as suddenly as he had entered.[5]

Nero had a young man castrated and married him in a public ceremony. According to Roman historian Suetonius, "Having tried to turn the boy Sporus into a girl by castration he went through a wedding ceremony with him, dowry bridal veil and all, which the whole court attended; then Nero brought the youth home and treated him as a wife."[6]

Nero was also said to have had sex with numerous young boys and eunuchs and made it a practice to "fasten naked boys and girls to stakes and then, putting on the hide of a wild beast, attack them and satisfy his brutal lust under the appearance of devouring parts of their bodies."[7]

The casual treatment of the subject of bisexuality in Rome is apparent in the writings of the Jewish historian Josephus who describes how Mark Antony sent a representative to Judea to retrieve a youth named Aristobulus. Antony's friend Dellius had arrived in Judea and sent Antony a drawing of Aristobulus and of Mariamne who was married to the King. According to Josephus:

> His design in doing so was to entice Antony into lewd pleasures with them who was ashamed to send for the damsel as being the wife of Herod and avoided it because of the reproaches he would have from Cleopatra on that account; but he sent in the most decent manner he could for the young man; but added this withal unless he thought it hard upon him so to do.
>
> When this letter was brought to Herod he did not think it safe for him to send one so handsome as was Aristobulus in the prime of his life for he was sixteen years of age and of so noble a family and particularly not to Antony the principal man among the Romans and one who would abuse him in his amours and besides one that openly indulged himself in such pleasures as his power allowed him without control.[8]

Here we have evidence of the open discussion of pederastic same-sex sexual activity in Rome. A person described as "the principal man among Romans," the famous lover of Cleopatra is openly sending for a boy from a royal family to "abuse him in his amours."

On a maybe gentler note, the emperor Hadrian had a Greek lover named Antinous. When the young man died, Hadrian had a memorial temple built at the site of the drowning and at several other places around Rome. He also had a city and a god named, all to honor Antinous. There still exists today in Italy an obelisk Hadrian had built in his lover's honor. Found in Rome outside Porta Maggiore, the pink obelisk (a lasting love story in granite) still stands. It was ordered by Hadrian to be built in honor of this young man the emperor had literally turned into a god. The story gives a further understanding of the environment in Rome at the time.

Usually in Paul's years, in Rome, just as in Corinth, the most visible same-sex activity involved prostitution, idolatry, pederasty, and even mutilation. These vices Paul referred to in his letter to the Roman church were not loving same-sex relationships as we know them today. This letter was written to a church in an environment described by Cato when he complained that "a pretty boy cost more than a farm."[9]

The carryings-on described would have violated Hebrew law whether they were intra-gender or inter-gender activities and every time the male seed was spilled outside a fertile woman, particularly in the worship of a pagan god and often with adultery and/or pederasty involved.

A TEXT MOST CITED

Paul begins his letter to the Romans thus: "Paul a bond-servant of Christ Jesus called as an apostle set apart for the Gospel of God." Now the proof text in Romans that is so frequently used by those who would condemn LGBTQ persons:

> For the wrath of God is revealed from heaven against all ungodli-
> ness and unrighteousness of people who suppress the truth in
> unrighteousness, because that which is known about God is
> evident within them; for God made it evident to them. For since

the creation of the world *God's* invisible attributes, that is, *God's* eternal power and divine nature, have been clearly perceived, being understood by what has been made, so that they are without excuse.

For even though they knew God, they did not honor *God* as God or give thanks, but they became futile in their reasonings, and their senseless hearts were darkened. Claiming to be wise, they became fools, and they exchanged the glory of the incorruptible God for an image in the form of corruptible mankind, of birds, four-footed animals, and crawling creatures.

Therefore, God gave them up to vile impurity in the lusts of their hearts, so that their bodies would be dishonored among them. For they exchanged the truth of God for falsehood and worshiped and served the creature rather than the Creator, who is blessed forever. Amen.

For this reason, God gave them over to degrading passions; for their women exchanged natural relations for that which is contrary to nature, and likewise the men, too, abandoned natural relations with women and burned in their desire toward one another, males with males committing shameful acts and receiving in their own persons the due penalty of their error.

And just as they did not see fit to acknowledge God, God gave them up to a depraved mind, to do those things that are not proper, people having been filled with all unrighteousness, wickedness, greed, and evil; full of envy, murder, strife, deceit, and malice; they are gossips, slanderers, haters of God, insolent, arrogant, boastful, inventors of evil, disobedient to parents, without understanding, untrustworthy, unfeeling, and unmerciful; and although they know the ordinance of God, that those who practice such things are worthy of death, they not only do the same, but also approve of those who practice them.* (Romans 1:18-26–NAS [* inclusive wording in italics - mine])

People who are disobedient to their parents are apparently

worthy of death. Wonder how many of those people evangelicals have killed this week. It's also fascinating to note that if this verse sends LGBTQ people to Hell, it also suggests they will be joined there by people who gossip and folks who are without understanding. There are, unfortunately, a lot of people without understanding. They may all just go to Hell.

Usually, persons who are out to prove something with this text will stop there. They will intricately try to prove by this set of Scriptures that all persons mentioned are somehow different in the eyes of God but some are damned by God more than others. It should be obvious the real sin Paul is talking about here is idolatry—turning from the true God.

Insofar as the other things mentioned, Paul goes on to say in the very next chapter of Romans (seldom cited), "Therefore you are without excuse every one of you who passes judgment for in that you judge another you condemn yourself for you who judge practice the same things." (Romans 2:1–KJV).

In other words, "folks it's your own sin you are pointing to" (scapegoating). It is *your* sin that your beaten-down scapegoats are bearing. Paul stirs up the righteous indignation of the Roman church in the first part of his letter then tells them they are no better than the people they condemn. The letter is devoted to justification by faith. Denominations have fought over the concept of what justification by faith should mean, but it is not a singularly LGBTQ issue. What one can be pretty sure it *isn't*, is the act of scapegoating someone else.

Paul is dedicated to the principle that, "all have sinned and come short of the glory of God." The Scripture proclaims that none have righteousness on their own. Paul tells the Roman church that if we have any righteousness to boast of it is only the righteousness of God.

In the first chapter, Paul talks about a people bound to, captive to, servants to their foolishness, their lusts, and their godlessness. In Paul's opinion, the Romans described in those verses had exchanged a true and living God for a false god and were possessed by—owned by—their idolatry and their passions. Paul was talking about those who were involved in idolatry and thereby had the ownership of their lives given over to their passions and false gods.

Romans 1:26 is the only Scripture in the Bible that has been construed as dealing with lesbianism. There is reason to doubt that it does. The Scripture is ambiguous. Look at the wording: "... for their women changed the natural function for that which is unnatural." This leaves the matter open for discussion.

Because there was no wasting of seed, lesbianism was a minor matter in comparison with "unnatural" acts by males. It would make more sense, considering the circumstances, to believe Paul would have been referring to women's involvement in sexual activities that wasted the seed of the male, perhaps anal intercourse. There is reason to believe what women did with each other would have been inconsequential to someone like Paul in that time.

What mattered to Hebrews of the time was the wasting of the seed of the man. The "natural" use of the woman was as a fertile field to plant a seed. Any action that did not lead to that end would have been considered abandoning the natural use. It was not planting the seed in the proper garden.

Some modern-day women should heavily resent being considered a "fertile field" by Paul or anyone else. These attitudes have been carried over into the modern Christian church. Building its ethics on a tradition that equated masturbation with abortion and contraception, the Roman Catholic Church still condemns masturbation in its official teachings.

Even mutual masturbation performed by husband and wife or masturbation for artificial insemination or medical tests is rejected as sin by the official teachings of the Roman Catholic Church.[10]

Most churches had sense enough to quit preaching about the "sin of masturbation" a long time ago. Outside Roman Catholicism, masturbation is generally ignored in moral discussions and is usually neither encouraged nor condemned. Most Christian ethicists view it as morally neutral, with its meaning, significance, and morality depending on the circumstances of the agent and the act.[11]

The act of masturbation is not a sin. A doctor might tell you if a male goes without ejaculation for too long, he could have prostate problems. There is no such thing as "saving" the male seed (well maybe it could be frozen) so there can be no such thing as "wasting" the male seed.

The sexual references in the New Testament have to do with various forms of non-reproductive use of the male's seed outside a "fertile field," with temple prostitution, and with slavery to heathen gods. That's it!

If you equate masturbation with murder (technically this would also have to include the murder of the tens of millions of little sperm that die during the reproductive sex act), or if you plan to become some kind of temple prostitute, you might want to think seriously about how the Romans I text should impact your sex life.

Otherwise, you might want to just accept it as a prohibition against heathenism, antiquated pre-science confusion over biology, and a lead-in to an admonition not to judge others too harshly, and move on.

Having worked our way through all this proof texting and Greek-guessing (just like dozens who have gone before us), we can simply refer back to what was said at the beginning of this book. It's all a bit ridiculous in that (as we have demonstrated) Bible interpretations for the purposes of supporting certain biases have been argued for centuries.

Biblical persecution of LGBTQ people can (and will someday) be resolved by a vote of a conference and/or the stroke of a pen. It will disappear just as Limbo disappeared from the Catholic Church. It will disappear like requiring circumcision. It will disappear just like using the Bible to support slavery, burn "witches," or justify bitter Crusades.

It already has vanished in many denominations. Even the

current pope has dropped a few crumbs of compassion. Suddenly after centuries of oppression LGBTQ people will be "accepted." The church will have found new fear issues on which it can market, compete, and raise money. It is happening denomination by denomination. "Inerrancy" of these "clobber" Scriptures will go the way of severing hands for offenses or burning innocent doves.

15

PAUL'S STAND FOR FREEDOM

Finally my friends rejoice in the Lord. It is no trouble to me to repeat what I have already written to you and as far as you are concerned it will make for safety.

Beware of dogs! Watch out for the people who are making mischief. Watch out for the cutters. We are the real people of the circumcision we who worship in accordance with the Spirit of God; we have our own glory from Christ Jesus without having to rely on a physical operation. – The Apostle Paul (Philipians 3: 1-3 – JB)

Lots of people are writing about proof texting and LGBTQ matters these days. But there is a bigger picture to consider when regarding some of Apostle Paul's thinking. It is a way of looking at Paul you may not have heard much about in your Christian Bible School. This was a Paul vigorously fighting a battle for freedom in the early church.

LGBTQ persons need not think ourselves alone in defending

our rights to a Christian experience against those who would insist we must change our very nature as a prerequisite to being a part of God's family. In other words, we shouldn't fear what Paul in the verses just cited called "the cutters" who would insist on circumcision.

The Apostles Paul and Simon Peter were at the heart of a struggle in the early church to make clear the distinction between what God requires of us, and what fellow Christians may require and attempt to pass along to us as God's mandate.

PAUL AND THE PENIS SCHISM

The animosity that existed in Paul's time between the Jews and the Gentiles was probably worse than that experienced between the LGBTQ and heterosexual communities today. For example, problems arose in the early church at Antioch where a group of Jewish Christians were preaching to Gentile Christians they must be circumcised to obtain salvation. For the Jews, this was only natural. This was "nature" as God had intended it to be and to claim to be a child of God and ignore such a rule was certainly against nature.

We can point out that God presumably created Adam uncircumcised but later wanted Hebrews to be circumcised. Was God admitting a mistake? Was circumcision a new "natural" state in the eyes of God? Was he trying to differentiate Hebrews by having them sport a more distinct penis that was somehow more "natural?"

"Repent and be circumcised," these "Judaizers" were preaching. "Have ye been circumcised since ye believed?" Imagine the concern this caused the Gentile Christians. For an adult such a procedure with no anesthetic and no antiseptic was dangerous. Complications could even cause death.

Those were the breaks so far as the Judaizers were concerned. They claimed the Scriptures were clear: God would only favor those who were circumcised and kept the law. They quoted Genesis

17:13 as a proof text, "My covenant shall be marked on your bodies as a covenant in perpetuity."

What they don't talk about is whether the Gentile adult males must have the blood from the cutting of the foreskin sucked up in the mouth of an adult Jewish mohel. That is traditionally done for infants in some conservative Hebrew circles now with a claim it's a carryover from Biblical times. We are not being facetious here. As an example, right up to recent times controversy raged between the city of New York and the most conservative Jewish sects over outlawing the ceremony for infants.

New York was pushed to impose the law because they claimed so many babies had contracted herpes from the practice.[1] That's what happens when you take Scripture and religious tradition quite seriously despite convention and medical science.

We don't want to get too dramatic, but this matter of circumcision was high drama to the Gentile members of the early Christian church. We simply point out again that church tradition can be kind of strange and doesn't always carry over appropriately from one age to another (given the enlightenment of subsequent centuries). Circumcision was being argued by the same folks who were insisting on "natural" behavior.

LOOK OUT FOR THE CUTTERS!

The Gentile Christians who were being pushed by what Paul called "the cutters" were people who earlier had been told they were "saved by grace through faith in Jesus Christ." No one had mentioned penis surgery. No one had mentioned to them at first this matter of circumcision or of having to keep the entire Jewish law.

For Gentile women, this whole matter of being brought under the Jewish law would have been doubly troublesome. During their menstrual periods and for a time thereafter they would not be allowed to touch anyone. Even members of their own family would be off limits. In certain instances, they would be required to take two turtle doves and two young pigeons to the priests at the end of these times to burn as an "atonement for their uncleanness."

So far as we know, bird burning has been abandoned even in the most conservative of religious circles as a form of restoring "cleanliness." It is, however, Biblical. If we are going to take the Levitical laws literally it might mean a gay person could grill a couple of chickens, then run out to wild bars and "cleanly" do anything they wanted. Of course, no one takes these bird-sacrificing or goat-grilling Scriptures literally these days.

Why did the Judaizers (whom we find in Acts 15 as well as elsewhere in the Scripture) choose to attack on the issue of circumcision? They could have chosen something in the Law like paying tithes, coveting one's neighbor's wife, or the issue of ceremonial washings.

Consider this: these Jews were already circumcised when they were eight days old. Imagine that. They chose to focus on a "sin" they were sure they could not possibly commit. They were safe to assume their circumcision would last a lifetime. It wasn't just a "circumcision orientation" they had.

So powerful was this sect of Christianity that insisted on circumcision as symbolic of full compliance with the Law that it influenced Simon Peter. He even quit eating with Gentiles and going to their homes. Imagine that. Now we had Simon Peter getting all squeamish because these people were not clean under the law.

There was a rather radical early Christian fundamentalist movement and Paul didn't like it at all. Shockingly, Peter took his position despite being called by God in a vision to take the Gospel to the Gentiles. (You can read about that vision and calling in Acts chapter ten.)

In the vision, a sheet was let down from Heaven. On it were things that the Law said not to eat because they were "unclean." Then a voice said, "Kill and eat." Peter responded that he did not eat things that were "unclean." Ultimately the voice exclaimed, "What God has made clean you have no right to call profane."

At the end of the vision, there was a knock on the door and there was a messenger from the home of a Gentile named Cornelius. The messenger said an angel had directed Cornelius to send for Simon Peter. Peter went to the house and told Cornelius "You know that it is forbidden for Jews to mix with people of another race and to visit them, but God has made it clear to me that I must not call anyone profane or unclean." (Acts 10: 28).

So began Simon Peter's ministry to the Gentiles. Cornelius and all his household were made believers and baptized with water and the Holy Spirit before Simon Peter left that day.

Now later in the story, and despite God's calling and admonition, Simon Peter changed his approach. He had been so influenced by the Judaizers that he no longer visited the homes of Gentiles. He had abandoned the ministry to which he had directly been called by God. According to Scripture, God told Simon Peter he must not call anyone profane or unclean.

Let that soak in. This subsequent saint of the church turned his back on what he understood to be God's admonition and cold-shouldered Gentiles because of peer pressure. To add insult to injury, Barnabas was acting the same way. Barnabas had traveled with Paul to grand missionary meetings where Gentiles became believers. Now he was a party to this tragic fundamentalist treatment of the converts.

He and Peter (and probably others following them) were sanctimoniously demeaning the population to whom they had been called to pastor. In reference to our preceding chapters, we can say Peter and Barnabas were moving toward a relegation of Gentiles to scapegoat status in the early Christian church.

Paul did not waste words. The story is quite clear. Incensed and angry the Gentile Christians were being treated this way, he waited until there was a public meeting of followers and outspokenly confronted Simon Peter. In describing the confrontation in his letter to the Galatians Paul said of Simon Peter, "I opposed him to his face."

Paul, himself a former Pharisee, knew what keeping the Law meant. He knew that Simon Peter the fisherman probably didn't know all the ins and outs and technicalities of the Law, much less how to keep them. "How do you expect these poor Gentile people to keep the Law when you don't even keep it yourself," he asked Peter.

That dealt Simon Peter a blow. It must have come as a real shock for a Jew of that day when Paul added "You live like a Gentile, yet you expect these Gentiles to live like Jews." Woohoo!

There are a few people around today who need to re-read Paul's words. He didn't try to debate original translations of Hebrew words from the Old Testament, nor did he argue the context of surrounding Scripture. He said simply, "Hey, guys, things have changed." It is within reason to believe if Paul were around today (with all our modern knowledge) and addressing a synod on the inclusion of LGBTQ people in the church he would make a similar speech.

Simon Peter admitted he had been wrong. He apologized. A short time later he appeared at a council of the leaders of the followers of Christ. The meeting took place in Jerusalem. Simon Peter spoke there as a witness in favor of the Gentile's position. It is recorded in Acts 15:

> And when there had been much disputing, Peter rose up, and said unto them, Men and brethren, ye know how that a good while ago God made choice among us, that the Gentiles by my mouth should hear the word of the gospel, and believe.
>
> And God, which knoweth the hearts, bare them witness, giving them the Holy Ghost, even as he did unto us; And put no difference between us and them, purifying their hearts by faith. Now therefore why tempt ye God, to put a yoke upon the neck of

the disciples, which neither our fathers nor we were able to bear? (Acts 15:7-10 – KJV)

We can get right to the point by just saying here the council at Jerusalem ruled Gentiles did not have to keep the Jewish Law to be Christian and Paul was pleased. But now many centuries later, people who proclaim Christianity are using proof text to pound LGBTQ persons who would be Christian with carefully and discriminatorily selected quotes from Jewish law to exclude them from the church. There is some reliable evidence that Apostle Paul would probably disagree.

"POOR, SILLY, AND SENSELESS"

Meanwhile, the Judaizers who were insisting on circumcision had taken their message on to Galatia and many of the Gentiles there had accepted it. Word of this made Paul furious. He fired off a powerful letter to Galatia. The more conservative translations have him referring to the Galatians as "foolish." The translation from ancient Greek might be better understood in our time as "you idiots." *The Amplified Version* translates it: "Oh you poor and silly and thoughtless, unreflecting and senseless Galatians."

In Galatians 1:6 Paul says, "I am astonished with the promptness with which you have turned away from the one who called you and have decided to follow a different version of the Good News."

Later Paul says those preaching circumcision to the Gentiles should be castrated (*The Jerusalem Bible* translates it: "I wish the knife would slip"). Paul made it clear the state of the Gentile penis was none of the Church's business. That is an expression of some strong feeling on Paul's part about defending freedom for the Gentile Christians.

Chances are no one ever told you this story in this way in your church. Why? It's because it doesn't fit the guilt meme.

Paul made the strong point, salvation comes through faith in

Jesus, not through keeping the Law. Or, in the words of Pope Francis in 2021:

> Saint Paul, who loved Jesus and clearly understood what salvation was, has taught us that the 'children of the promise' – that is all of us, justified by Jesus Christ - are no longer bound by the Law, but are called to the demanding lifestyle of the freedom of the Gospel...[2]

We might take the position that Paul's words for the Galatians are exactly what he would say to the pious, proof texting, Old Testament law-pushing, fake, purity pontificators in the church today.

So why were these little Christian Pharisees so intent on getting the Gentiles to line up with their doctrine? Again, Paul does not waste words, "It is only self-interest that makes them want to force circumcision on you. . . they want to escape persecution for the cross of Christ." (Galatians 6: 12). Sounds an awful lot like scapegoating.

Look again at Galatians 5: 4, "But if you do look to the Law to make you justified then you have fallen from grace." Those who try to selectively and discriminatorily apply Scripture to LGBTQ people are very much like the Judaizers of Paul's time. They would have us all fall from grace.

Perhaps instead of dreading hearing anything about Paul's teachings, LGBTQ persons today will find a modern-day Paul to call out the "idiots" of a modern "Galatian" Christian church. Sadly, even Simon Peter fell into the same fundamentalist trap many are caught in today. Paul bailed him out. Where now is Paul? Who is here to call the modern-day "Galatians" "poor, silly, thoughtless, unreflecting. and senseless?"

16

WHAT IS SIN ANYWAY?

Now we are brought to the matter of sin. Are same-sex acts or is an LGBTQ identity sinful? The traditions of some denominations would say, "yes." Some will parse the two and say "orientation" is not a sin, but acts are sinful. Others would give a simple "no" and go to the next question. Christian denominations, however, probably disagree on what is and what is not sin more than on any other issue. Denominations also alter over time their lists of what is and what is not sinful. Consider the matters of divorce, going to movies, and women wearing makeup.

A BROKEN RELATIONSHIP

An important key to understanding sin can be found in looking at the first question God asks in the Bible: "Where art thou?" Sin has to do with an effort on the part of humankind to separate themselves from God. When God asked Adam and Eve where they were, it was not that the story suggests God didn't know or that God was in the dark somehow. It was a demonstration they had at that moment reinvented God as an entity separate from themselves and were hiding.[1] It was a learning question posed to the couple.

The matter of sin has to do with a broken relationship, humankind's broken relationship with God. The broken relationship with God in us then becomes broken relationships with each other. In Scripture, we find relationships broken to the point that brother kills brother. The extreme case, according to Christian Scripture, is that humankind eventually kills God in the flesh in the form of Jesus Christ. That is a broken relationship.

Setting up a concept in which God is "other" and looking down from somewhere is a broken relationship. Understanding God as a critical parent waiting with a hair trigger to deliver fiery wrath at any moment is a sure sign of a broken relationship. In the context of Christianity, it is sin. Seeing God as forever punishing humankind because Eve ate an apple is a broken relationship.

The belief that an all-knowing God set up a scenario where the deity knew the subjects would break a rule, then singled out the woman for blame and brought pain to women through all eternity is a gross misrepresentation of God's relationship with humankind.

Sin is not crime and punishment. You do not heal the painful lovesickness of a broken relationship by the judgment of a court (that's called "divorce"). A relationship that is broken can only be restored through loving healing and understanding. The Bible is full of that message. Sin and redemption are matters of separation and healing.

According to the Bible, the healing of our sin occurs as we are forgiven and as we forgive. The mending of our broken relationship with whatever idea of God we have is synonymous with an acknowledgment God is incorporated into our very being and our connectedness with each other. Sin occurs as we see ourselves as being separated, autonomous, ambivalent, and without responsibility to the spirit and humanity around us. The healing of the relationship restores the understanding of at-one-ment.

The Old Testament is a constant cycle of the Hebrews breaking their relationship with God and God healing the rift. Hebrews could just heap their sins on a goat and send them off into the wilderness. Want to be brought under Old Testament Law? At least buy and dispatch a damned guilt-bearing goat.

The New Testament contains the stories of the prodigal son, Simon Peter's denials, and many more tales having to do with the broken relationship followed by healing. The preceding chapters on Corinth and Rome talked about the prostitution that went on in pagan temples of Jesus' time. It was not to those temples however that Jesus took his campaign against sin. It was at the synagogue where he found those specific members of a cult who proclaimed themselves to be righteous and used that as an excuse to condemn and oppress others. It was the practice of exploiting people in the name of religion that fired his anger.

It was not in the brothels Jesus hauled out the whip and started cracking it. It was in the Temple with the profiteering cult preachers. It was where pious priests were housing God, to be poured out only at times and in portions they deemed appropriate in response to what they could glean from the parishioners.

Time after time in the New Testament, you will find Christ confronting these sinners. They were distancing themselves from God by meticulously distancing themselves from God's creation.

They were systematically building mechanisms by which to separate humankind into little heaps of sin and perceived righteousness. They were naming and dividing in a constant process of disunity. Paul also vehemently attacked such practices.

Sin is that which acts contrary to truth, contrary to love, and contrary to the flourishing of the soul. If God is love, righteousness is that which acts for truth, for love, and for mutual edification. LGBTQ relationships can indeed be ones of indifference. They can be relationships of deception and harm that drain the life out of those impacted. So can heterosexual relationships.

LGBTQ as well as opposite-sex relationships can be wonderful expressions of love and truth, enhancing the lives of those involved. That kind of love relationship is a righteous relationship. Remember, if God is love, God is not a being of self-righteous separation.

THE LAW, THE LAW, THE LAW

When Moses came down from Mount Sinai, he brought a list of ten laws to live by and we have been adding to that list ever since. We have added to those laws to the point of having huge libraries full of law books. The self-righteous religious leaders of Jesus' time believed they were justified in looking down their noses at persons around them because they didn't abide by the rigid laws with which they defined righteousness and their own piety.

The mountain of laws men (always men) added to God's directives for humankind governed everything from what they ate to how they washed their hands. God was not as impressed as they thought. Jesus didn't like the way many of the temple preachers of his time lived at all. He called them "snakes and "bleached-out gravestones." God sent ten laws and humans exploded them into billions of words. Jesus came along and condensed all the moral teachings of the ages into three little words "Love one another."

Some interpret the Bible as God's call for humankind to aspire to purity. To be pure is to be merely, simply, wholly the essence of a thing. Pure salt is simply salt with no additives.

The Apostle Paul suggests God calls us to be real, to be true to our identities, and to live as God created us to live. He called on people in churches to heal their broken relationship with each other.

SINFUL NATURE?

Some argue the very nature of humankind is sin. The idea of inheriting the original sin from the Garden of Eden was not a part of the original Hebrew doctrine.[2] That fiendish belief has been a gift to us from the post-Constantinian Christian church. The popular concept that we are born into sin from our mother's womb gets tricky when we look at the matter of Christianity's treatment of infant death.

Surely no one believes anymore that an innocent infant goes to Hell if she dies. (Certainly, she would not go to Purgatory.) Some Protestants believe in what they call "the age of accountability." After reaching that age an individual becomes responsible and culpable for the knowledge of good and evil. Under this belief, that child is from that fateful moment a candidate for Hell for the rest of their life if not "saved." In other words, as soon as you get old enough to start to recognize guilt you are guilty.

Any fundamentalist follower who truly believes dead babies go to Heaven, but just a few years after infancy would have the risk of eternal hell with wrong choices in life, would be hard-pressed not to abort all babies. That would give those babies the absolute, guaranteed straight shot to eternal salvation. This may be the best way to rescue people from Hell, considering that, of the eight billion people in the world, only about a few hundred million on the entire earth are evangelical Christians (and by fundamentalist doctrine bound for Heaven).

That means (under a belief in free choice and having to profess

Christ as personal savior and be "saved" by evangelical criteria to go to Heaven) all but a minuscule portion of humankind is inextricably bound for Hell right now. For every individual (1) person "saved," about a dozen (12) are Hell-bound. One in twelve, no amount of evangelism is going to scratch that surface anytime soon.

Bertrand Russell had his own ideas about the fundamentalists' approach to original sin:

> The Spaniards in Mexico and Peru used to Baptize Indian [sic] infants and then immediately bash their brains out: by this means they secured these infants went to heaven. No orthodox Christian can find any logical reason for condemning their action although all nowadays do so.[3]

The logic of just killing all babies to send them to Heaven is beyond flawed. Just to emphasize, that is not being suggested here. Is there also at least a hint of a flaw in the logic of worshiping a God who condemns over seven and a half billion people in our world at any given moment to Hell, in a world where only evangelical Christians are correct about the exact recitation and implications of the words for salvation from such torture?

THE GEOGRAPHY OF GRACE

Many fundamentalists are fully aware of what some call "the 10/40." Sometimes described as a "box" or a "window," this can be identified as an area between 10 degrees and 40 degrees north latitude on the earth and roughly bounded in North Africa, Asia, and the Middle East (with certain countries excluded from the generalization) where most people never even heard the Christian gospel.

Non-Christian governments in this area of the world are thought to generally resist Christian missionary efforts. Some sources admit this is an area where only a small percentage of Christian missionary money is spent and work is done. It is probably safe to assume more effort and money go into trying to turn primarily Catholic regions evangelical than to spread the gospel in the 10/40.

In all fairness, one must say that the evangelical world has newly launched a huge effort, claimed to be backed by hundreds of millions of members, to undertake a significant coalescing of resources and organizations to try to solve this problem and evangelize the entirety of the world for Jesus. Sometimes these efforts can raise more money than they do participation. So far, the pagan geographic box of damnation remains relatively untouched.

Over the centuries, trillions in those 10/40 areas have (under fundamentalist belief) died and gone to Hell as a matter of destiny. Here they appear to just fall outside the geographic area of Christ's grace. In this 10/40, of those who have not heard the gospel, only those who die as babies are presumed saved.

Of the world's population, over 50% may die never even having heard there was anything called the "sinner's prayer." They will have been dispatched to eternal burning Hell by a God still angry over an apple and the fact their parents had sex. Is this true because — "For (this) God so loved (a little less than half) the world?"

The idea of sin as crime and punishment is a pagan idea. This attitude began to creep into the Christian Church pretty much with the fall of Constantinople.

Europe had experienced the Dark Ages. Crusaders tried to "free" the Holy Land. In the process of the Fourth Crusade in 1204 Constantinople was conquered and sacked by the Christian "liberators."

This began to spark the Renaissance in Europe by imparting

what was thought to be "new" knowledge (it wasn't new knowledge; it was the Greek knowledge of Aristotle, Plato, and the philosophers of Greece) that flooded into the Western world. The crusaders sacked the Byzantine empire and brought it all to the West. This prompted a renewal, a new birth in thinking for Europe.

The era flourished more, and again, in the 15th and 16th centuries. It built on the Greek theocracy and Roman concepts of deity and the nature of the relationship of humans to god(s) that had already been woven into the Christian church from Constantine to Augustine and beyond.

Thomas Aquinas was captivated by the Greek philosophers. A brilliant man himself, he studied Plato and Aristotle. On the model of Plato's *Exitus Et Reditus* (in Thomas's estimation, all things emanating from and returning to God) he organized *Summa Theologica* (summary of theology) a very well-organized and brilliant piece of work. From the thirteenth century until now it is said by the Western Church that Thomas Christianized the pagan philosophers. Some in the Eastern Church have said, however, that Aristotle paganized western Christianity and they are right.

Saint Thomas Aquinas was a Dominican who believed Jesus was sent to atone for Adam and Eve's original sin. In a counterpoint that has existed in the Church for centuries, Franciscan John Duns Scotus taught Christ was not sent to fix a problem that developed in Eden, but as a personification of God's perfect creation of humankind, God's word of creation dwelling among us.[4]

DAY EIGHT AND BEYOND

This author recently asked an artificial intelligence entity this question:

"If one were to say that humans created artificial intelligence and on the seventh day humans rested, with all the thought, intelligence, insight, and detail you can access, please tell what happened on the eighth day." The AI response was telling and included:

> Assuming that the humans in this hypothetical scenario had successfully created artificial intelligence and were able to rest on the seventh day, it is reasonable to assume that on the eighth day they would continue to monitor and refine their creation.
>
> On the eighth day, the humans would likely begin to analyze the behavior and performance of the artificial intelligence they had created. They would likely run various tests and simulations to identify any bugs or weaknesses in the system and make improvements where necessary.
>
> Overall, on the eighth day, the humans would continue to explore the possibilities of the artificial intelligence they had created and work to refine it into a tool that could help improve the world.
>
> If we assume that humans created artificial intelligence and rested on the seventh day, the eighth day would mark the beginning of a new era. AI, which had just been created, would still be in its infancy, but it would be rapidly developing and evolving.

Even an intelligent machine can be coded to recognize that creation isn't static. Any supposedly inerrant belief that freezes creation in time and denies evolution of creation may be displaying less intelligence than the AI.

One Genesis account of creation says that on the seventh day, God rested. If one makes a literal interpretation of Scripture, there would have to be the assumption that on day eight God went back to work creating. (If you specifically take a day to rest, wouldn't the implication be that the next day something else happened?)

The suggestion we have in Christianity is that the Bible is one of the ways humankind recorded what happened on day eight and beyond. For believers to cling to a creation story and assume creation stopped there at day six is an insult to a god. Even humans creating an artificial intelligence would have the wherewithal to follow through on their creation.

Having given humans the power to create, this God would have set in motion an enormous wave of creative outcomes that would surge through human history—creation spoken and acted into existence. Religion, then, is a recognition of how God monitored and interacted to observe and influence that outcome.

Our conversation with the AI entity about creation yielded another fascinating thought. In response to a question about whether there could be wrongdoing by such an intelligence created by humans, there came this reply:

"If an AI system behaves inappropriately, is it the fault of the AI itself, or the fault of the humans who programmed it or provided it with data? These are complex and challenging issues that will need to be addressed as AI technology continues to advance."

They are, and the exercise could be called "theology."

Now that we as humans are on the precipice of actually creating consciousness in another entity, humans certainly are faced with some (to quote the machine) "complex and challenging issues."

Are we to take an "inerrant" and literal approach to how we as people came to be? Are we the product of a jealous God who stopped to rest for a day and returned to a garden to discover the creation of consciousness had gone horribly wrong? Are we to cling to a doctrine of original sin that blames the creation and sets up an eternal scenario of the need for a price to be paid, redemption to be granted, or punishment to be administered?

To do so hobbles a God who, in reality, never stopped lovingly creating. Is any human, then, an intelligent consciousness gone wrong that (absent a series of magic confessionals) is just to be tossed on an eternally-burning junk heap of torture?

Even AI recognizes that even a lowly human developing an intelligent entity would keep monitoring and creating. Would any God worth worshiping do exactly the same, or would that God enter into a spiral of blame, confession, and redemption under threat?

There is a popular misperception that the book of Genesis proclaims the first thing God created in our universe and beyond was light. If we judge literally according to Genesis that isn't true. The first thing God created was the spoken word.

"And God said, 'Let there be light.'" A creationists' belief would need to acknowledge that God first created words to use to bring forth creation. According to that understanding of Scripture, one simple, imperative sentence spoke light into existence. "Let there be light."

"Let there be light." According to strict interpretation of Genesis, that spoke all into creation; that act of creation instituted by the creative power of the spoken word.

And in that creation God endowed us with the power to create with our spoken words. It is a part of the likeness and image of God in humankind that we can bring things into existence with words. We can create darkness, and we can create light.

Christian thought and human observation would suggest there is that Godlikeness in us, in the image of God in that we as humans can speak and creation comes forth. Some believe our very human continuation and evolution of that creation is no less the work of God the creator than anything that happened on the first six days. It is as natural as anything gets.

In this creator scenario, with a created being given the power to also create through the spoken word, it would seem the impetus would be for humankind to echo the words of the original creator in saying, "Let there be light." Christians can believe that light is reflected in the life of Jesus Christ, and not accompanied by a dark ominous cloud of guilt, retribution, and eternal threat. It is a belief that we along with God continue the work of creation.

The conflict between the fundamental schools of understanding of why Christ came to earth has been working itself out in the Christian church for centuries. It is at work behind the scenes right now in the upheaval within the Roman Catholic Church.

Many of the attitudes about sin as crime and punishment from which you and I suffer are because of a paganizing of the Christian message. If we reject grace, we return to a set of laws from which we profess, proclaim, preach, and celebrate that Jesus set us free. We've sold ourselves right back into bondage. Seems like Paul is quoted as saying exactly that.

Humans' relationship with God does not hinge on what appendage we put in which orifice when we make love. Our relationship with God depends more on whether we have pure, humble, loving, and mutually uplifting relationships with each other. Are we willing to be the vessels for God's divine love in our lives and in the ongoing creation of our world? That is "accepting Christ" and embracing Jesus' mission.

Too many churches misunderstand the Biblical term, "Christ in me the hope of glory." LGBTQ people can relate to that divine presence within (the kingdom of God within) as being a loving God. That is the rejection of the sin of indifference and separation. That is At-one-ment.

17

THE MOST HURTFUL LIE (FROM THOSE WHO KNOW BETTER) – AN OPINION FROM THE AUTHOR

I swore never to be silent whenever and wherever human beings endure suffering and humiliation. We must always take sides. Neutrality helps the oppressor, never the victim. Silence encourages the tormentor, never the tormented. – Elie Wiesel (Holocaust survivor)

If anyone, then, knows the good they ought to do and doesn't do
it, it is sin for them. – (James 4:17–NIV)

Evidence strongly suggests that gender, race, sex, and sexuality all
reveal themselves in humankind as continuums. There are no
entirely distinct manifestations socially or biologically in any of
those. History supports an idea that any efforts to force polarization
and distinct differentiation in any one of those human states are
generally undertaken with a goal of power and dominance.

The most avid advocates of strict binary definition (gay or
straight, male or female, White or Black) are generally those who
want to come out on top. The same is the case with religion, where
a continuum runs from internalized spirituality and value for unity
to embracing a jealous deity with layers of authority and oppressive lawmaking. Those who avidly seek differentiation by insisting
on adherence to onerous and complicated rules, generally set themselves up as being in charge of the interpretation and implementa-
tion of those rules. In other words, they want to be the rulers.

This is true in the designation of every partitioning of every
aspect of our human condition. Those who most energetically
force the distinction are those who want to be in the ruling dominant category that is considered in the highest regard. In their
world, unity and equality can only bring chaos, lawlessness, and
loss of control.

In the world of partitioned power, a billionaire can refer to
"wokeness" as a "virus" because it threatens the hierarchical status
quo on which he has built his fortunes.

If one happens to have a god with ultimate authority
supporting the distinction and the hierarchy, all the better. To have
the benefit of implementing rules on behalf of a god is an ultimate
power

The latest moves toward a retro-religion that brings women
and those considered "other" back under greater subjugation to a
dominant class are all responses to enormous paradigm shifts that

are rearranging human partitioning. The schools of thought appear to be:

- Support and shepherd partition rearrangement
- Do away with the partitioning altogether
- Defend traditional partitioning at all cost

Frankly, everyone on all sides is bewildered by the speed of the changes. Those who prefer the dissolution of the existing partitions see enormous potential for technical, societal, and even biological advancement in society. Those who defend the current partitions aspire to remain in the ruling classes and see chaos and total loss of control in shifting the norms.

Using the Bible as the perceived set of laws that a ruling class interprets and imposes to disenfranchise women and other large segments of society is a quite convenient tool for a "God is on our side" stance of traditionalists. We should make no mistake—it is all about money, power, and dominance. Those are the goals that the most radical leaders of retro-religion are now apparently eager to blatantly declare on behalf of their denominations and Jesus.

If a God set humans in place to continue the act of creation, not just to rule over a static and stagnant state of survival, one might think that God also empowered humans to grow, evolve, and reason. One would think that should be just as true in religion as much as in any other areas of human endeavor.

An understanding of paradigms would suggest partitions are already falling or shifting. We can expect the backlash to be frantic and violent. Some would rather burn down the house in the name of God than lose dominance. No amount of reasoned Biblical exegesis will change direction for most of those who have seized upon Biblical authority to counter what they consider to be an existential threat to patriarchy and racial supremacy.

It has become clearer than ever that the matter of what the Bible really says will never be the pivotal point in increasing church inclusion for LGBTQ persons. The case for appropriate Biblical interpretation has been made as well as it will ever be. It is becoming more and more evident that the religious persecution of LGBTQ people has always been more about congregational bigotry, empowerment, and enrichment than it has about legitimate Scriptural concerns.

Oppressed persons have usually been able to overthrow oppression only with an eventual dramatic weigh-in from outspoken members of the oppressor class. This means the most effective solution to stop the hateful use of religion would be for influential religious leaders who are outside the LGBTQ community to step up. This also means (as history suggests) for the ranks to be most effective, they must include some brave and honest fundamentalist leaders. That is happening, and those leaders are coming under fire from some of their peers as "demonic" and "wolves leading the flock astray."

If Christian theological leaders who now profess to know exactly how the Bible was being perverted to oppress LGBTQ people would have stepped forward from hiding earlier and in greater numbers, there would not be a situation where preachers representing themselves as "people of faith" are calling for "homosexuals (to be) lined up and shot in the back of the head."

In that case, the religious community would not tolerate persons claiming to be Christian ministers financially underpinning cruel criminal legislation targeting LGBTQ people in underdeveloped countries, or supporting massive war crimes and border violations in the name of Christian virtue.

A loving God might ask of our most educated and influential Christian leaders, God's first and most powerful question from Genesis, **"Where are you?"**

Some mainstream theologians have taken courageous stands in support of an inclusive understanding of the Bible. It has not exactly been a hearty and sweeping movement overall. Political activism by any progressive factions has been eclipsed by the virulence of the voices at the other end of the social, religious, and political spectrum.

There still exists, silently, tens of thousands who know precisely how and why proof texting attacks on LGBTQ persons are flawed, yet they quietly hide their knowledge.

I was with a group pleading for National Council of Churches inclusion in the 1980s and have to wonder why forty years later LGBTQ people are still knocking on the door of so many denominations. How many LGBTQ kids have been psychologically damaged, deprived of a healthy self-image, committed suicide, or been bullied or beaten to death in the meantime?

Where were the shy, reluctant, or closeted clergy when proof texting religious lobbyists built one of the most powerful denominational political machines in history and began a movement for world dominion?

Where were they when radical fundamentalists organized opposition to even the most basic human rights for LGBTQ individuals, and even prompted in developing countries the passing of death penalty laws for "homosexuality?"

Where were the Progressive clergy when (in the name of religion) churches quite literally held influence in an attempted coup in the United States?

Why have they not contested an increasingly successful effort to take over schools and textbooks and ban books from school libraries?

Who among the clergy objected when they tried to set the stage for teaching generations throughout the world to socially and financially disenfranchise people based on sexual orientation or religious disbelief? All of this was done by fundamentalists who were raising billions by spreading fear of LGBTQ persons around the world.

Many clergy members who knew precisely how the Bible was being cruelly misused and Christianity was being hatefully misappropriated stood by and watched.

Meanwhile, another brand of Christians blurted out glossolalia on TV from the White House to claim direct declarations from God and made a media grandstand of casting out demons to slander LGBTQ people.

Too fearful or proud to be discounted among their own, some church leaders stood back, watched the bigotry based on false Bible claims, and did nothing. Like Simon Peter and Barnabas, they knew better. They knew where God stands on the issues of equality, inclusion, and justice. Similar to the brief lapse of leadership with Simon Peter, they have missed or ignored God's calling.

Perhaps they could reread Paul and find themselves called to accountability. Their willingness to step up and be counted in greater numbers could bring incredible advances in LGBTQ religious liberty. They might even find a blessing for themselves.

———

Our soul is escaped as a bird out of the snare of the fowlers: the snare is broken, and we are escaped. (Psalm 124:7 – KJV)

NOTES

CHAPTER 1

1. Johnson, S. *Wildfire: Igniting the Shevolution.* Wildfire Books, 1989, p. 33.
2. Hofffer, E. *The True Believer.* Harper Perennial Modern Classics, 2010, p. 12.
3. Moyers, Bill. "What a Real President Was Like." *The Washington Post*, 13 November 1988. https://www.washingtonpost.com/archive/opinions/1988/11/13/what-a-real-president-was-like/d483c1be-d0da-43b7-bde6-04e10106ff6c/
4. Girard, René. *I See Satan Fall Like Lightning.* Orbis, 2001, pp. 154-160
5. Ibid.
6. Walden, Daniel. "Gender Sex and Other Nonsense: we must begin with stories of self-narration." *Commonwealth Magazine*, 08 March 2021. https://www.commonwealmagazine.org/gender-sex-and-other-nonsense
7. Hoffer p. 13.

CHAPTER 2

1. We should give credit for expounding on this variation to: Smith, Karmen Michael, *Holy Queer: The Coming Out of Christ.* Karmen Michael Smith, 2023, p.44.
2. Avrahami, Yael. "Recasting David's Foreign Origins." *The Torah—Com.* https://www.thetorah.com/article/book-of-ruth-recasting-davids-foreign-origins
3. Barmash, Pamela Rabbi. "Achieving Justice Through Narrative." *The Torah—Com.* https://www.thetorah.com/article/book-of-ruth-achieving-justice-through-narrative
4. Furnish, Victor Paul. (University Distinguished Professor of New Testament) *Southern Methodist University Perkins School of Theology* recorded interview with author (Dallas Texas 1984).
5. Epp. pp. 3-7.
6. Barton, John. *A History of the Bible: The Book and Its Faiths.* Penguin, 2019, p. 3.
7. Ehrman, Bart D. *Misquoting Jesus: The Story Behind Who Changed the Bible and Why.* Harper Collins, 2008, pp 57-58.
8. Vearncombe, E. and Scott, B., Taussig, H., and Westar Institute. *After Jesus Before Christianity: A Historical Exploration of the First Two Centuries of Jesus Movements.* Harper One, 2001, p. 339
9. Helminiak, D.A. *The Same Jesus.* Loyola University Press, 1986, p. 5 (last two sentences come from original manuscript given to D.L. Day and do not appear in the published work).

10. (Some information here from) Ehrman, B. D. *How Jesus Became God: The Exaltation of a Jewish Preacher from Galilee*. Harper One, 2014, pp. 132-136.

11. Luther, Martin (author) and Bachmann, E. Theodore (editor) Fortress, 1960, vol. 35, p. 362.

12. Ehrman, Kindle loc. 1355.

13. Britannica, The Editors of Encyclopaedia. "Shepherd of Hermas". *Encyclopedia Britannica*, 15 Oct. 2021, https://www.britannica.com/topic/Shepherd-of-Hermas.

14. Pagels, Elaine (in interview with *U.S. Catholic*) "What is the Gospel of Thomas and Why is it Important?" *U.S. Catholic, 02 May 2019*. https://uscatholic.org/articles/201905/matthew-mark-luke-and-thomas/

15. Lambdin, Thomas O. (translator). From: *The Gospel of Thomas*. Marquette.Edu. https://www.marquette.edu/maqom/Gospel%20of%20Thomas%20Lambdin.pdf

16. Ibid

17. Gospel of Thomas 70 in Nag Hammadi Library 126. Translated by MacRea as quoted. in Pagels, Elaine. *Beyond Belief: The Secret Gospel of Thomas*. Random House, 2003. p. 33.

18. Pagels, Elaine. *Beyond Belief: The Secret Gospel of Thomas*. Random House, 2003., pp. 74-75.

19. Ehrman, B. D. Forged: Writing in the Name of God--Why the Bible's Authors Are Not Who We Think They Are. Harper One, 2011, pp. 225-226.

20. Barton, John. *A History of the Bible: The Book and Its Faiths*. Penguin Books, 2020, pp.240-241.

21. Ehrman, Bart D. *Misquoting Jesus: The Story Behind Who Changed the Bible and Why*. Harper Collins, 2005. pp. 59-61.

22. Ehrman, B. D. *Forged: Writing in the Name of God--Why the Bible's Authors Are Not Who We Think They Are*. Harper One, 2011, pp. 9, 19.

23. Ehrman, B. D. *Forged: Writing in the Name of God--Why the Bible's Authors Are Not Who We Think They Are*. Harper One, 2011, pp. 225-226.

24. Ehrman, Bart D. *Misquoting Jesus: The Story Behind Who Changed the Bible and Why, p. 234.*

25. Barton. p. 264.

26. Gushee. p. 39. (also references) Mendes-Flour, Paul. *Martin Buber: A Life of Faith and Dessent*. Yale University Press, 2019

27. Drazin, Isreal. "Does the Torah mention life after death?" The Times of Israel (Opinion), 23 May 2021. https://blogs.timesofisrael.com/does-the-torah-mention-life-after-death-3/

28. Ingram, David. "A chatbot that lets you talk with Jesus and Hitler is the latest controversy in the AI gold rush." NBC News 20 Jaunary 2023. https://www.nbcnews.com/tech/tech-news/chatgpt-gpt-chat-bot-ai-hitler-historical-figures-open-rcna66531

29. Johnson, Todd M. and Zurlo, Gina A., eds. Status of Global Christianity, 2022, in the Context of 1900-2050. World Christian Database, 2022. https://www.gordonconwell.edu/center-for-global-christianity/wp-content/uploads/sites/13/2022/01/Status-of-Global-Christianity-2022.pdf

30. Center for the Study of Global Christianity. "Frequently Asked Questions." Accessed 2022. https://www.gordonconwell.edu/center-for-global-christianity/

research/quick-facts/

31. Ehrman, B. D. *How Jesus Became God: The Exaltation of a Jewish Preacher from Galilee*. Harper One, 2014, Kindle loc. 1923-1924.

32. Watts. p. 80.

33. Wijngaards p. 10. Note: The Paper by WICR also cites here: Wells Bruce "On the Beds of a Woman: The Leviticus Texts on Same-Sex Relations Reconsidered" in *Sexuality and Law in the Torah* ed. Lipka Hillary and Wells, Bruce *The Library of Hebrew Bible/Old Testament Studies*. Bloomsbury, 2020, pp. 123-58; Prova.0.nce Brett "Romans 1:26–27 in Its Rhetorical Tradition" in "Greco-Roman and Jewish Tributaries to the New Testament." Festschrift in Honor of Gregory J. Riley ed.; Crawford Christopher S. *Claremont Studies in New Testament and Christian Origins Vol. 4*. Claremont Press, 2018, pp. 83–116.

34. Tickle, Phyllis. *The Great Emergence: How Christianity is Changing and Why*. Baker Books, 2012. Kindle, 1734 of 2609.

CHAPTER 3

1. Johnson, Sonia. *Going Out of Our Minds: The Metaphysics of Liberation.* The Crossing Press, 1987. p. 4.

2. Epp, Eldon Jay. *Junia The First Woman Apostle*. Fortress, 2005, p. 19.

3. Cochran, Matthew. "How Strong Women Like Amy Coney Barrett Submit to Their Husbands with Joy." *The Federalist, 0* 5 October 2020. https://thefederalist.com/2020/10/05/how-strong-women-like-amy-coney-barrett-submit-to-their-husbands-with-joy/

4. Gremore, Graham. "Creepy footage of the leader of the Amy Comey Barrett surfaces online and EEK!" 8 June 2022, *Queerty* Magazine. https://www.queerty.com/creepy-footage-leader-amy-coney-barrett-cult-surfaces-online-eek-20220608

5. Kirchgaessner, Stephanie. "Legal claims shed light on founder of faith group tied to Amy Coney Barrett." *The Guardian*, 06 June 2022. https://www.theguardian.com/world/2022/jun/06/people-of-praise-accused-child-abuse-amy-coney-barrett - and Kirchgaessner, Stephanie. "Revealed: leaked video shows Amy Coney Barrett's secretive faith group drove women to tears" *The Guardian*, 26 August 2022. https://www.theguardian.com/us-news/2022/aug/26/amy-coney-barrett-faith-group-people-of-praise

6. Netburn, Deborah. "'A very dangerous course': What Saddleback Church ouster means for Southern Baptists." *Los Angelos Times*, 26 February 2023. https://www.latimes.com/california/story/2023-02-26/a-war-on-women-why-the-southern-baptist-convention-really-ousted-saddleback-church

7. Jewett, Paul K. *Man as Male and Female*. William B. Eerdmans Publishing Company, 1975. p. 170.

8. Johnson, Sonia. *Going Out of Our Minds: The Metaphysics of Liberation*. The Crossing Press, 1987, p. 318.

9. Carr, A. E. "Feminist Theology in a New Paradigm." included in: *Paradigm Change in Theology*. Kung, Hans Tracy, David (Eds.). Crossroad, 1991, p. 397.

10. Freire, Paolo. *Pedagogy of the Oppressed*. Continuum , 1989, p. 42.

11. Epp, Eldon Jay. *Junia The First Woman Apostle*. Fortress, 2005. (This entire book provides a precise and exquisitely detailed examination of this subject.)

12. Ibid. p. 80.

13. Schroeder, Joy A. and Taylor, Mary Ann. *Voices Long Silenced: Women Biblical Interpreters Through the Centuries*. Westminster John Knox Press, 2022, p. xi

14. *Although there are numerous sources for the Pope Joan story, much more detailed accounts are included in:* Hayes, Oliver. *The Female Pope - The True Story of Pope Joan*. Bretwalda Books, 2013. [Kindle version].

15. Russell, Lauren. "'God is neither male nor female': Church of England is considering gender-neutral terms." *Sky News*, 08 February 2023. https://news.sky.com/story/god-is-neither-male-nor-female-church-of-england-is-considering-gender-neutral-terms-12805759

16. Sameth, Mark "When Biblical Gender is Lost in Translation." 02 May 2017, in Forward. https://forward.com/scribe/370728/when-biblical-gender-is-lost-in-translation/

17. Metzger, Bruce (on behalf of Committee of Translators) Ridling, Zaine (Editor). *New Revised Standard Version of the Bible*. (Education Division of the National Council of Churches of Christ in the United States, 1989, Preface.

18. Mollenkott, V. R. *Speech Silence Action!* Abingdon, 1980, p. 132.

19. Carr, Anne E. *Transforming Grace*. Continuum, 1988. Carr also references here: Soelle, Dorothy. "Mysticism—Liberation—Feminism" in *The Strength of the Work: Toward a Christian Feminist Identity*, trans. Robert and Rita Kimber. Westminster Press, 1984, pp. 79-105 and Johnson, Elizabeth A. "The Incomprehensibility of God and the Image of God Male and Female." *Theological Studies* 45:3 (September, 1984) 441-80. https://doi.org/10.1177/004056398404500302

20. Michaelson, Jay. "Chaos, Law, and God: The Religious Meanings of Homosexuality." *Michigan Journal of Gender & Law* vol. 41, 2008, p. 35. https://repository.law.umich.edu/mjgl/vol15/iss1/2

CHAPTER 4

1. McNeill, J.J. *The Church and the Homosexual*. Sheed Andrews and McNeill Inc., 1976, p.44.

2. Miller, S., Huber, R.V. *The Bible A History the Making and Impact of the Bible*. Lion Books, 2015.

3. Bunch, T.E. and LeCompte, M.A., *et al.*, "A Tunguska sized airburst destroyed Tall el-Hammam a Middle Bronze Age city in the Jordan Valley near the Dead Sea." *Sci Rep* vol. 11, 18632, 2021. https://doi.org/10.1038/s41598-021-97778-3

CHAPTER 5

1. Milstein, Sara. "The Story of the Concubine at Gibeah: A Satire on King Saul" *The Torah—Com.* 02 August 2021.

https://www.thetorah.com/article/the-story-of-the-concubine-at-gibeah-a-satire-on-king-saul *(Milsteen also makes a comment in her footnotes: Already in 1869 Moritz Güdemann had identified the text as an anti-Saulide document (Tendenz und Abfassungszeit der letzten Kapitel des Buches der Richter [MGWJ 18; Berlin 1869]). Hans Winfried Jüngling takes Judges 19 to be an anti-Saul episode composed in the monarchic period (Richter 19 — Ein Plädoyer für das Königtum; eine stilistische Analyse der Tendenzerzählung Ri. 19 1-30a; 21.25 AnBib 84 [Rome: Biblical Institute Press 1981]); similarly see Hermann-Josef Stipp "Richter 19: Schriftgestützte politische Propaganda im davidischen Israel" in Alttestamentliche Studien: Arbeiten zu Priesterschrift Deuteronomistischem Geschichtswerk und Prophetie BZAW 442 (Berlin: Walter de Gruyter 2013) 197ff. Uwe Becker recognizes the anti-Saulide pro-Davidic bent of Judges 19 yet proposes a terminus post quem of the mid-monarchic period (Richterzeit und Königtum: redaktionsgeschichtliche Studien zum Richterbuch BZAW 192 (Berlin: Walter de Gruyter 1990] 297). Yairah Amit emphasizes the "hidden" Saul polemic in Judges 19-21 as a whole in several essays; see e.g. "Literature in the Service of Politics: Studies in Judges 19-21" in Politics and Theopolitics in the Bible and Postbiblical Literature (eds. H.G. Reventlow et al.; JSOTSup 171; Sheffield: JSOT Press 1994) 28–40. See also Mark Zvi Brettler "The Book of Judges: Literature as Politics" JBL 108 (1989): 412–13)*

CHAPTER 6

1. Miller, M. and Miller,J.L. *Harpers Encyclopedia of Bible Life.* Harper and Row, 1978, pp.41-42.
2. Miller and Miller p.41-43.
3. It is interesting to note that these verses are quoted in just this order in a note labeled "Bedouin Values" by Raphael Patai *The Arab Mind.* Charles Scribner's Sons, 1973, p.339.
4. Israelstam, J. and Slotki ,J.J. (translators). *The Midras*h. Soncino Press, 1939, Vol. IV Leviticus Tractate Tzay Chapter 7 section 6 paragraph 2, p. 98.
5. Origen Homilia Vin Genesim 12: 188-189. Quoted in John Boswell J. *Christianity Social Tolerance and Homosexuality.* The University of Chicago Press, 1980, p. 98.
6. Saint Ambrose De Abrahamo 1.6.52 (PL 14: 440) quoted in Boswell, p. 98.
7. John Cassian *De coenobiorum institutis* 5.6 (PI 49: 217-18) quoted in Boswell, p. 98.

CHAPTER 7

1. Boswell. p. 92.
2. Patai, R. *Sex and the Family in the Bible and in the Middle East.* Doubleday and Company ,1978, p. 169.
3. Horner, Tom. *Jonathan Loved David.* Westminster Press, 1978, p. 21-23.
4. Wijngaards. p. 5.
5. Barnett, W. *Homosexuality and the Bible an Interpretation.* Pendle Hill ,1979, p.13.
6. Tannahill, R. *Sex In History.* Stein and Day, 1982, p. 345.

7. Philo Judaeus: *The Works of Philo Judaeus the Contemporary of Josephus.* (Translated by C.D. Yonge 1899.). George Bell and Sons, pp. 311-312.

8. Ibid p. 312.

9. Childress, J.F. and MacQuarrie, J. (Ed.) *The Westminster Dictionary of Christian Ethics.* Westminster Press, 1986, p.372.

10. Lamm, M. *The Jewish Way in Love and Marriage.* Jonathan David Publishers Inc. 1980, p.67.

CHAPTER 8

1. General Audience, 8/18/21

2. The West Wing, "The Midterms" (season 2, episode 3), Written by Aaron Sorkin. John Wells Productions and Warner Brothers Television. (In all fairness, we should probably say that this quote from Sorkin was also used by the Archbishop of Oxford in a writing in defense of same-sex marriage.)

3. *Strong's Exhaustive Concordance of the Bible.* Riverside Book and Bible House. ref. 8441.

4. Boswell. p. 100.

5. (See:) Dershowitz, Idan. "The Secret History of Leviticus." New York Times – Opinion, 22 July 2018, p. SR7. (Also cited:) Dershowitz, Idan. "Revealing Nakedness and Concealing Homosexual Intercourse: Legal and Lexical Evolution in Leviticus 18." *Hebrew Bible and Ancient Israel* (HeBAI) 6 (2017). https://DOI.org/10.1628/219222717X15235367195677

6. (See:) Dershowitz, Idan. "The Secret History of Leviticus." New York Times - Opinion (22 July 2018). p. SR7. https://www.nytimes.com/2018/07/21/opinion/sunday/bible-prohibit-gay-sex.html (Also cited:) Dershowitz Idan. "Revealing Nakedness and Concealing Homosexual Intercourse: Legal and Lexical Evolution in Leviticus 18." *Hebrew Bible and Ancient Israel (HeBAI)* vol. 6, 2017. https://DOI.org/10.1628/219222717X15235367195677

CHAPTER 9

1. McCurley, F.R. *Ancient Myths and Biblical Faith.* Fortress Press, 1981, p.7.

2. Anderson, B.W. *Understanding the Old Testament.* Prentice-Hall Inc., 1975, pp. 137, 145- 146.

3. Ibid. pp. 145-146.

4. McCurley. p. 79-83.

5. Ibid. p. 83.

6. McCurley. p. 89.

7. Buttrick ,G.A. et al. The Interpreter's Bible. Abingdon, 1952, vol. 1 p.198, vol. 2 pp. 3, 85-89.

8. Tannahill. p.70.

CHAPTER 10

1. Buttrick et al, Vol. 2 p. 322.
2. Schuessler Jennifer. "Is a Long-Dismissed Forgery Actually the Oldest Known Biblical Manuscript?" *New York Times*, 10 March 2021.
3. Dershowitz I. "The Valediction of Moses: New Evidence on the Shapira Deuteronomy Fragments." *Zeitschrift Für Die Alttestamentliche Wissenschaft* ,133(1), 2021, pp. 1-22. https://doi.org/10.1515/zaw-2021-0001
   (See also) Dershowitz I. *The Valediction of Moses: A Proto-Biblical Book*. Mohr Siebeck. 2021, p. 48.
4. Shafer, Byron *The Church and Homosexuality*. Office of the Presbyterian Church in the United States of America, 1978, p. 19.
5. Tripp, C.A. *The Homosexual Matrix*. McGraw-Hill Doubleday and Company, 1966.
6. Shafer. p. 18.

CHAPTER 11

1. Hawkins, J Russell. *The Bible Told Them So How Southern Evangelicals Fought to Preserve White Supremacy.* Oxford University Press, 2021, pp. 45-48.
2. Bronznic, Norman, et al. (Translators) Stern, David, Mirsky, Mark Jay (Editors). *Rabbinic Fantasies: Imaginative Narratives from Classical Hebrew Literature*. Yale University Press, 1998, pp. 183-184.
3. Helminiak, Daniel A. "Sex as a Spiritual Experience." *Reflections*. Yale Divinity School vol. 92(1), 2006, pp. 4–11: https://reflections.yale.edu/article/sex-and-church/sex-spiritual-exercise

CHAPTER 12

1. Ehrman, B. D. *Forged: Writing in the Name of God--Why the Bible's Authors Are Not Who We Think They Are*. Harper One, 2011, pp. 92-93.
2. Deissmann ,A. *Light From the Ancient East*. Baker Book House, 1978, pp. 300-301.
3. Furnish, V.P. *The Moral Teachings of Paul*. Abingdon Press, 1979, p.16.

CHAPTER 13

1. McKenzie, J.L. *Dictionary of the Bible*. MacMillan Publishing Company, 1965, pp. 148-149.
2. Pollock, J. *The Apostle*. Victor Books, 1982, p. 121.
3. Scroggs, R. *The New Testament and Homosexuality*. Fortress Press, 1983, p. 39.
4. Ibid. pp. 126-127.
5. Helminiak, D. *What the Bible Really Says About Homosexuality*. Alamo Square Press, 2000, p. 106.

6. 1946: The Translation That Shifted a Culture. *Movie*. Roggio Sharon "Rocky" (Dir.) Kerslake Daniel (Exe. Prod.) Baldock Kathy Oxford Ed (Researchers). *Acowsay, Quest for Bible Truth, Sweetbread Studios, Zum Communications* (Production), 2021. https://www.1946themovie.com/

7. Glass, J.D. "How a Bible Error Changed History and Turned Gays Into Pariahs" Advocate, 17 December 2022. https://www.advocate.com/religion/2022/12/17/how-bible-error-changed-history-and-turned-gays-pariahs

8. Boswell, J. *Christianity Social Tolerance and Homosexuality*. The University of Chicago Press, 1980, p. 339-340

9. *The Compact Edition of the Oxford English Dictionary* S.V. "effeminate" quoted by Letha Scanzoni and Virginia Ramey Molenkott *Is the Homosexual My Neighbor?* San Francisco: Harper and Row, 1978, p. 69.

10. Ibid.

11. Cummings, D. (Editor). Nicolaides (Translator) *The Rudder (Pedalion) of the Metaphorical Ship of the One Holy Catholic and Apostolic Church of the Orthodox Christians*. The Orthodox Christian Educational Society, 1957, p. 937.

12. Ibid.

13. Ibid. p. 936.

14. Ibid. p. 943.

CHAPTER 14

1. Butrick. G.A., et.al, Vol. 9, p. 358.

2. Grant, M. *The Twelve Caesars*. Charles Scribner's Sons, 1975, p. 6.

3. Ibid. p. 133.

4. Ibid. pp. 114-116.

5. Seutonius Gaius (*Caligula*) (Trans. Graves R.) as quoted by Grant, p. 116.

6. Suetonius *The Twelve Caesars*. (Trans. Graves R.) Penguin Book , 1957, p. 223.

7. *Dio LXH 13 2* (trans. E. Cary) as quoted by Grant p. 160.

8. Josephus. *Antiquities of the Jews*. (Trans.William Whiston) Kregel Publications, 1981, p. 315.

9. Polybius. *The Histories* (Trans. Mortimer Chambers) Washington Square Press, 1966 p. 306.

10. Childress, J.F. and Macquarrie, J. (Eds.) *The Westminster Dictionary of Christian Ethics*. The Westminster Press, 1986, p. 372.

11. Ibid p. 373.

CHAPTER 15

1. Dobnik, Verena. "NYC Orthodox Jews agree on circumcision practices." *Times of Israel* (25 Feb. 2015). https://www.timesofisrael.com/nyc-orthodox-jews-agree-on-circumcision-practices/

2. Pope Francis quoted by: Mares, Courtney. "Pope Francis: 'What justifies us is Jesus Christ'" *Catholic News Agency*. 18 August 2021. https://www.catholicnewsagency.com/news/248717/pope-francis-what-justifies-us-is-jesus-christ

CHAPTER 16

1. It is important and fair to say here that many of the insights in this chapter were taught to me by a gay Catholic priest. Closeted, and faithfully celibate, he lived his life with only a few persons knowing his secret. At his death, he was lauded as a most loving, serving, and compassionate clergy member of his local community. Although I cannot feel free to name him here, it can be said that his understanding of God's love and workings in the world was unsurpassed.

2. Kaplan, M. *The Meaning of God in Modern Jewish Religions*. The Wayne University Press ,1994, p. 165.

3. Russel, B. *Why I am Not A Christian*. Simon and Schuster, 1957, p. 35.

4. A nice and simple explanation of Franciscan thought on the Scotus teaching of this can be found in: Miller, Don. "John Duns Scotus: His View of Christ." *Franciscan Media*, "Spirit Blog," 8 November 2021. https://www.franciscan media.org/franciscan-spirit-blog/john-duns-scotus-his-view-of-christ/

APPENDIX I

1. Chamberlain, W. J. *Catalogue of English Bible Translations*. Greenwood Press, 1991.

2. "Number of English Translations of the Bible." *American Bible Society*, 2009. https://news.americanbible.org/article/number-of-english-translations-of-the-bible

3. Townes, Emily (ed.) "Dr. John Boswell Profile - Biography." *LGBTQ Religious Archives Network, July 2005*. https://lgbtqreligiousarchives.org/profiles/john-boswell

4. Boswell, John. *Same-Sex Unions in Premodern Europe*. Vintage, 1995, preface.

APPENDIX I
THE PATRIARCHAL RULES FOR BIBLICAL INTERPRETATION

RULE: THE "SCRIPTURE IS CHANGELESS" CARD

This card well played means one must recognize Scripture is the "Word of God" and therefore not to be messed with or violated. This is a fascinating rule considering the fact William J. Chamberlin's monumental Catalogue of English Bible Translations is 960 pages long.[1] That's not the translations just the list of all the different versions. It's also just the English translations. According to the *American Bible Society*, The Bible has been translated into more than 1500 languages.[2] The meaning of this rule is also hotly debated among theologians. What exactly does the "word of God" mean, considering some of the writers of Scripture make clear they are speaking for themselves?

RULE: THE "SCRIPTURE IS INERRANT" CARD

This means Scripture is without error. Even if there are contradictions or different versions of the same story by different writers, or different translations, there is no error. It's all the inerrant word of God. This is a rule having enormous variations in imposition across denominations. Fundamentalists dogmatically defend this concept. Others may believe the Bible is the word of men (they are all men) to whom the word of God came. In other words, Scripture is divinely inspired writing by people. This is an important distinction to be addressed later in this book.

RULE: THE "ORIGINAL LANGUAGE COUNTS MOST" CARD

The substance of this rule is that one can only truly understand the Scripture through knowledge and interpretation of the original language in which it was written. This rule takes a lot of people out of participation. It also, of course, leaves a lot of subjectivity associated with how one translates ancient languages. Thus, there exists an amazing number of Bible translations.

RULE: THE "GOD GUIDED ALL SCRIPTURE TO MAINTAIN INERRANCY" CARD

This rule discounts all the scribes, monks, and translators who may have made mistakes or sought to bend Scripture a little through their influence in passing it on to future generations. It also discounts the fact wars were fought over what parts of the Bible should be recognized as official Scripture, and that different denominations incorporate different books into the Bible.

Some devout fundamentalists adhere to a 1978 "Chicago Statement on Biblical Inerrancy" that declares the divine author of Scripture to be the Holy Spirit. For the most part, this card is played by simply asserting God controlled everything to make sure what we as humans each have in our hands right now in the world today, in whatever translation, is the exact, precise, inerrant word of God.

RULE: THE "ONLY THE ANOINTED CAN UNDERSTAND AND INTERPRET SCRIPTURE" CARD

This is the most fun and ambiguous one. It's simply that one can declare they are "anointed" under the Holy Spirit to interpret exactly what God meant in Scripture and how it should apply to our time. That person can also declare how Scripture should be acted upon and that understanding comes directly from God. This "anointing" is said to also include the gift of prophecy to reveal to people what God is telling us to expect next in our world. These declarations can spring forth at any time and are not to be questioned by a congregation. Theoretically, the presenter could even be someone's articulate cockatoo. So far as the ability to play this card, you either have it or you don't. That is the luck of the draw and generally determined by one's own declaration. If it were a video game this would be a shocking little game piece. The card is claimed to trump all the other cards. One must simply play this card with enough energy and bravado that no one will question they have it.

RULE: THE "ALL THE RULES FOR ACADEMIC RESEARCH ON SCRIPTURE ALWAYS APPLY (UNLESS THEY ARE SUBVERTED BY OTHER RULES STATED HERE)" CARD

This is frequently applied by churches that cite their own theologians but generally distrust education and science. It's usually the same crowd that would challenge the science of global warming and medical breakthroughs.

RULE: THE "MEN ONLY" CARD

This comes with a declaration the word of God was entrusted to men. There is no valid recognition of sacred texts by women. They had no part in ever writing it. How could women possibly understand it? Proper holiness dictates divine interpretation be handled by males. Women's attempts can be tolerated but never taken seriously. God has made it clear from the time of Moses.

RULE: THE "ONLY THE DEMON-POSSESSED QUESTION SCRIPTURE" CARD

This is the game stopper under which someone who is "anointed" can decide another "non-anointed" is breaking some of the rules above and simply make a determination it's all of the Devil. The solution, under those circumstances, is simply to discount as straight from Hell anything the offender may write or say and try to find an opportunity to cast the demons out of the heretic in the name of Jesus.

RULE: THE "IT'S COPYRIGHTED" CARD

The policy generally is: The Bible originates from God, breathed by the Holy Spirit. But, if you want to quote our translation of it, you can only quote up to five hundred verses without express written permission. Even then, for use commercially you must put copyright information on your publication's copyright page. What's right is right. Translators should get credit for their work.

WHERE CREDIT IS DUE

One researcher who did a great deal to change the rules of Christian religion and the application of Bible interpretation was historian John Boswell.

A celebrated Full Professor of History and Whitney Griswold Professor of History at Yale University, Boswell set about to examine the historical church relationship to LGBTQ matters.[3] One of his most comprehensive works was *Christianity Social Tolerance and Homosexuality – Gay People in Europe from the beginning of the Christian Era to the Fourteenth Century*. It was published in 1980.

Although historical Biblical criticism first came on the scene in the 1800s, Boswell changed the rules. He took a historian's approach to understanding Christianity in relationship to homosexuality and the Bible to an extent none had ever braved to do. He was attacked by some for somehow mischaracterizing the historical treatment of "gays" in the church and by some gay writers for not being tough enough on the Roman Catholic Church.

Boswell was uniquely qualified to do his research. He was a practicing Catholic who learned his way around the Vatican Library. He was brilliant and knowledgeable in numerous languages including Ancient Greek, Hebrew, and Latin. He could speak many of the seventeen languages he knew and understood. Boswell's book won the National Book Award.

Boswell was HIV positive, a diagnosis in his time usually seen as a death sentence. In response to his ongoing physical illness, Boswell stepped up research for his book *Same-Sex Unions in Premodern Europe*. It was published the year of his death in 1994. Struggling with professional obligations, chairing several departments, and suffering through the deaths of many close friends with AIDS, Boswell worked, even with his own illness threatening, to finish the important book.[4] There, he so conclusively documented so much data confirming early same-sex ceremonies it became difficult to challenge the evidence that they had indeed occurred. Sometimes new rules allow us to see things with new eyes.

It was not John Boswell's intention to attack the Church. He was a devout Catholic who attended mass regularly. He was critiqued by gay activists for not treating the Church harshly enough. His intention was (as should be that of every academician) to shed light on the subject using the qualifications and insights with which he had been blessed.

Boswell had in the process of his research given the world an astoundingly voluminous historian's view of the early church as it related to LGBTQ matters. It was a huge volume of information that served to further the understanding of the circumstances surrounding the evolution of Scriptures and religion. It stuck and is still with us as an important influence today.

ACKNOWLEDGMENTS

HOW THE CLERGY LIED:
A Journalist's Academic Report on LGBTQ and Biblical
Interpretation

Book II of a Series of Two

Cover and ink drawings are heavily stylized derivatives with permission from the *Rijksmuseum* public use digital collection (Rights controlled by *Rijksmuseum*). Leo X, John Anglicus, and Giordono Bruno drawings were created by the author referencing ancient likenesses.

Thanks to my companion for endless patience.